MW00790596

Leadership Strategies for Successful Schoolwide Inclusion

Leadership Strategies for Successful Schoolwide Inclusion

The STAR Approach

by

Dennis D. Munk, Ed.D.
Carthage College
Kenosha, Wisconsin

and

Thomas L. Dempsey, M.S.Ed.
Lake County Regional Office of Education
Grayslake, Illinois

·P A U L·H·
BROOKES
PUBLISHING Co.®

Baltimore • London • Sydney

Paul H. Brookes Publishing Co.
Post Office Box 10624
Baltimore, Maryland 21285-0624
USA

www.brookespublishing.com

Copyright © 2010 by Paul H. Brookes Publishing Co., Inc.
All rights reserved.

"Paul H. Brookes Publishing Co." is a registered trademark
of Paul H. Brookes Publishing Co., Inc.

Typeset by Integrated Publishing Solutions, Grand Rapids, Michigan.
Manufactured in the United States of America by
Victor Graphics, Inc., Baltimore, Maryland.

The individuals described in this book are composites based on the authors' experiences. In all instances, names and identifying details have been changed to protect confidentiality.

Purchasers of *Leadership Strategies for Successful Schoolwide Inclusion: The STAR Approach* are granted permission to photocopy the blank tool forms in Chapter 6. None of the forms may be reproduced to generate revenue for any program or individual. Photocopies may only be made from an original book. *Unauthorized use beyond this privilege is prosecutable under federal law.* You will see the copyright protection notice at the bottom of each photocopiable page.

Library of Congress Cataloging-in-Publication Data

Munk, Dennis D.
    Leadership strategies for successful schoolwide inclusion: the STAR approach / by Dennis D. Munk and Thomas L. Dempsey.
        p.   cm.
    Includes bibliographical references and index.
    ISBN-13: 978-1-59857-089-2 (pbk.)
    ISBN-10: 1-59857-089-7 (pbk.)
    1. Inclusive education—United States.   2. Special education—United States.   3. Students with disabilities—Education—United States.   4. School management and organization—United States.   I. Dempsey, Thomas L.   II. Title.

    LC1200.M86 2010
    371.9'046—dc22   2010026876

British Library Cataloguing in Publication data are available from the British Library.

2014   2013   2012   2011   2010

10   9   8   7   6   5   4   3   2   1

Contents

About the Authors vii
Foreword   *William Bursuck* ix
Preface xi
Acknowledgments xiii

1 The Context for Inclusive Education 1

Perspective on Inclusive Education
The Context for Inclusive Education
Historical Context: Research and Discourse on Inclusion
Leadership and the Quest for Inclusive Education
Elements of Leadership for Inclusive Education
Wrapping Up and Looking Ahead
Recommended Resources
References

2 The STAR Leadership Strategy 15

Setting the Tone
Translating Research into Practice
Arranging for Collaboration
Reflecting on Processes and Outcomes
Implementing the STAR Leadership Strategy
Wrapping Up and Looking Ahead
Recommended Resources
References

3 Positive Influences on Inclusive Education: Principals, Peers, and Parents. 37

Principal Leadership
Roles for All Administrators
STAR Organizer for Principal Leadership
Peer Friendship and Support
STAR Organizer for Maximizing Peer Supports
Parent Involvement
Parents' Questions About Your Inclusive Program
Maximizing Parents' Involvement
STAR Organizer for Maximizing Parent Involvement
Wrapping Up and Looking Ahead
Recommended Resources
References

4 Leadership in the IEP Process: Going Beyond Procedural Compliance 57

Common Themes
IDEA Guidelines and the IEP

Leadership and the STAR Organizer
Wrapping Up and Looking Ahead
Recommended Resources
References

5 **Current and Evolving Practices with Implications for Inclusive Education** **79**

Maximizing Access to the General Curriculum
Universal Design for Learning
Response to Intervention
Wrapping Up and Looking Ahead
Recommended Resources
References

6 **Implementing STAR Organizer Activities: Tools to Expedite Your Work** **101**

Creating a Snapshot of Inclusion at Your School or District (Tool 6.1)
Creating a Vision Statement (Tool 6.2)
Applications of the STAR Organizer (Tools 6.3–6.5)
Sample Professional Development Survey (Tool 6.6)
Parent Survey Description (Tool 6.7)
IEP Meeting Feedback (Tool 6.8)
Sample Program Monitoring (Tool 6.9)

Index 123

About the Authors

Dennis D. Munk, Ed.D., Professor of Education, Carthage College, 2001 Alford Park Drive, Kenosha, Wisconsin 53140

Dr. Munk earned his Ed.D. in special education from Northern Illinois University in 1994 and has worked in human services and special education settings for 28 years. Dr. Munk published a text on grading practices for students with disabilities in 2003, has authored more than 30 chapters and articles, and has served as a reviewer for several journals. His research background includes data-based studies on a multitiered model for reading instruction and assessment and grading practices for included learners. He has provided professional development to school leaders on a variety of topics related to inclusive practices and has consulted with a state educational agency on the preparation of preservice educators for inclusive settings.

Thomas L. Dempsey, M.S.Ed., Educational Consultant, Lake County Regional Office of Education, 19525 West Washington Street, Grayslake, Illinois 60030

Mr. Dempsey has been practicing in the field of special education for 38 years as a classroom teacher, administrator, and consultant. Since 1991, he has served in leadership roles (e.g., Director of Special Education/Pupil Services) in districts striving to provide effective inclusive education. Mr. Dempsey has organized, developed, or delivered professional development on all or most of the topics addressed in this book. He has also served as adjunct faculty to special education preparation programs and is serving as a consultant with a regional office of education. Mr. Dempsey provides technical assistance to schools in the areas of school improvement, response to intervention (RTI), and the individualized education program (IEP) process.

Foreword

As we approach the 35th anniversary of the Individuals with Disabilities Education Act (IDEA), there are reasons to be optimistic about prospects for students with disabilities receiving a free appropriate public education. IDEA 2004 (PL 108-446) guarantees full access to the general education curriculum for 99% of students with disabilities. Even the 1% of students with disabilities who have the most significant learning challenges are expected to meet state standards, albeit it at a more functional level. More students with disabilities are participating in their state's high stakes assessments than ever before. Furthermore, IDEA demands that the quality of education for students with disabilities be judged not just from the standpoint of whether or not schools follow the appropriate process; schools must show that students benefit educationally from their special education services. Lastly, there is the clear expectation that evidence-based practices be a crucial part of both general and special education.

If I were a "glass half-full" type of person, I'd be feeling pretty good right now. But, alas, I am not; it is indeed difficult to know whether or not these changes will result in positive outcomes for students with disabilities. In large part, success for students with disabilities will depend on the actual level of access they have to the general education curriculum. Certainly, one aspect of this accessibility is physical; students with disabilities need to be physically present in general education classrooms in order to benefit academically and socially from what occurs there. Yet, as Munk and Dempsey point out in Chapter 1, the percentage of time students with disabilities spend in general education has actually plateaued over the last 10 years. Still, if we've learned one lesson in the years since IDEA was passed, it's that physical access by itself is not sufficient. Indeed, it's the quality of education that students with disabilities receive that counts, and, in this area as well, our schools have been found wanting. Postschool outcomes for students with disabilities continue to be a concern. Part of the problem is that demands for accountability are pushing schools in competing directions; content covered too often takes precedence over content learned. On a recent visit to Washington, D.C., I observed that the conversation on Capitol Hill had shifted noticeably from talk of "highly qualified" teachers to talk of "highly effective" teachers. It appears unlikely that the demands on schools and teachers will abate in the near future; in fact, demands to close the achievement gap are likely to increase, while resources to make change are likely to decrease. Sadly, these demands may overshadow the needs of students with disabilities, particularly at a time when fewer and fewer dollars are made available for education. Worse, the federal government may face increasing pressure to lower expectations for students with disabilities.

In the roughly 4 decades since IDEA was originally passed, we have seen the growth of special education into a mature field with its own teaching standards, professional organizations, research, journals, conferences, and federal dollars. Charting a separate course has by and large been a good thing. We have been able to provide the level of advocacy needed to bring public attention to the needs of students with disabilities. We have also been able to develop a foundation of evidence-based practices (e.g., curriculum-based measurement; uni-

ix

versal design; systematic, explicit instruction, to name a few) that would not otherwise have been developed. That said, charting a separate course in the environment of high accountability and ever-shrinking resources just described may no longer be tenable. The time for more systemic solutions that meet the needs of all children, with and without disabilities, is upon us. The mantra that what's good for students with disabilities is good for all children, while not a new refrain, can resonate in today's educational environment. Enter Munk and Dempsey and their STAR approach to implementing evidence-based inclusive practices.

That Munk and Dempsey have chosen inclusive practices as the basis for their focus on school reform makes sense. The tenets of inclusive practices such as shared responsibility, high expectations, universal screening, progress monitoring, collaboration, individualized instruction, and evidence-based practice, to name a few, are relevant for all learners, be they at risk, average, or high achieving. But these practices are not new. What's new here is a systemic approach linking the implementation of these evidence-based practices to all levels of the school leadership hierarchy, with special emphasis on the school principal. As Munk and Dempsey say, implementing and sustaining effective inclusion requires a schoolwide commitment and must not be viewed as a "special project driven by the vision and energy of select individuals."

As a professor of special education, a large part of my job is offering graduate classes for practicing teachers. In the many class discussions I have led on the topic of implementing research-based practices, the topic of school change is inevitably raised, and it is difficult to think of a single instance when the critical role of the principal in initiating and sustaining change hasn't come up. Indeed, an effective principal is the *sine qua non* of school change.

For inclusive practices to become an essential component of school reform, school leaders must be firmly committed to the belief that all students are entitled to a free appropriate public education and that the responsibility for providing that education is shared by everyone in the school community, teachers and parents alike. Yet, while belief in an approach is necessary for change to occur, it is not sufficient. Change is as much about process as outcomes, as there are many forces at work intent on maintaining the status quo. Administrators need a well articulated and organized game plan to carefully, unambiguously, and with a sense of urgency put the system in place. A noteworthy feature of Munk and Dempsey's book is that they communicate the process for implementing effective inclusive practices in such an eminently understandable way. The STAR strategy is indeed a memorable heuristic that makes the process of implementing inclusive practices explicit and memorable. In STAR, the authors have truly captured the "big ideas" involved in implementing inclusive practices; namely, setting the tone, translating research to practice, arranging for collaboration, and reflecting on outcomes and processes. In this book, Munk and Dempsey have carefully operationalized each step in STAR and have clearly delineated a process for change from planning, to implementation, to perhaps the most essential component of all: evaluation.

The 20th century was a time of great gains for children with disabilities. Whether or not those gains can be sustained and extended in the 21st century will depend on the quality of leadership in our schools. After reading Munk and Dempsey's book, I feel more optimistic; my glass is half full again. I am hopeful that their book will be read, taken to heart, and used to guide practice so that I may continue pouring.

William Bursuck, Ph.D.
Professor, Specialized Education Services
University of North Carolina at Greensboro

Preface

Before undertaking this book, we had a number of opportunities during the 1990s and beyond to collaborate professionally on schoolwide initiatives or individual cases involving inclusive practices. We also shared an interest in jogging and began to meet regularly at the local running paths in a never-ending quest for the perfect trail that only goes downhill (still looking). Our runs were punctuated with conversation about what we were observing and learning about supporting included students in our roles as school administrator, teacher educator, consultant, and researcher. Together, we enjoyed a multidimensional perspective that allowed us to compare notes and learn from each other's experiences. And, of course, we could not resist seeing similarities in what it takes to commit to both exercise and inclusive education—attempting to forecast and prepare for what usually prove to be unpredictable conditions; enduring the moments of "wind in your face"; sound management of resources (nutrition and good shoes); and the ability to see the longer term benefits of your efforts. And inclusive education, like exercise, becomes less work and more enjoyable when done consistently, as part of a natural routine.

While the literature and discourse regarding inclusive education often focused on specific issues or practices, our collective experiences taught us that putting all of the pieces together required leadership and a commitment to ongoing problem solving. We reflected on our own opportunities for leadership and took notice of what worked for others. Exemplars were those teams and individuals who shared an underlying belief that inclusion in the general education setting had inherent value; that learners with special needs should be held to a high standard, even when they were not working at grade level; that general educators and special educators should share expertise and responsibility for educating all learners and demonstrate a willingness to ask, "Is it working?" and make changes when the answer was, "No." It became clear to us that effectiveness was the result not of a single practice or strategy, but rather in the coordination of many "thrusts" in a way that made sense to educational teams, learners, and their parents. Also evidenced was a tendency for districts or schools to focus on adopting concurrent, new initiatives, sometimes without consideration of how they would impact current practices, or fit into an overarching mission for the school. What seemed to be missing was a framework for making decisions about what was working and what was needed. Thus, we sought to design a framework and process that brought together recommendations from the professional literature (a research base), successful practices of exemplars, and our own insights from a combined 70 years of experience.

The STAR leadership strategy was designed to provide both the structure and flexibility to allow its use at different levels of a school's leadership hierarchy. The four practice areas—setting the tone, translating research into practice, arranging for collaboration, and reflecting on processes and outcomes—embody the issues and practices that are needed to begin or sustain inclusive education. In choosing to pursue a leadership strategy, we are also acknowledging that one of the most challenging tasks school leaders face today is not access to information, but rather managing multiple sources of information and sometimes contradictory initiatives against a backdrop in which public scrutiny of academic achievement is higher than ever. We also perceived it to be important that a strategy encompass responsibilities typically carried out by all levels of school operation, from school board to individual teacher to parent. The literature on leadership supported our notion that leadership should be distributed, not centralized, and that all stakeholders should play a part.

The criteria we set for what would evolve into the STAR leadership strategy were ambitious. Such a strategy would have to be robust enough for use by experienced school leaders with substantial background in inclusive education, while also explicit enough for fledgling administrators ready to embrace inclusive education in their school. Toward that goal, we have presented the strategy in different formats and with varying levels of detail with the assumption that it can be utilized in many ways and by different levels of school leadership. The STAR organizer provides a template that prompts users to consider what they are currently doing, and what they should do, in each of the four practice areas. The organizer can be utilized for strategic planning, program evaluation, or tracking the activities of small groups or teams. We have also provided guiding questions to prompt users to attend to specific practices within each of the practice areas. The questions are designed to steer users toward recommended practices that are described within each chapter. We also present STAR formatted as a tool for self-assessing what evidence is available to answer each question and what action is needed to improve in each area.

Setting the tone occupies the initial position in STAR, and we would assert that establishing a clear mission and vision is the place to begin building an inclusive program. However, we do not perceive a need to approach the remaining three practice areas in any particular order, and would urge users to consider working in all three areas simultaneously. Some users may perceive reflecting on processes and outcomes (the *R* in STAR) as the logical place to begin, and most users will recognize that many leadership activities overlap practice areas. Users can elect to focus on all four practices areas, or on individual areas, and although this book focuses on inclusive education, the same areas of practice, and many of the guiding questions, are equally relevant for implementing any schoolwide initiative. This feature of the strategy should be appealing to users who have expertise and experience and are seeking ideas for fine-tuning their programs and establishing sustainability.

We hope that the STAR leadership strategy and related information and tools in this book will provide a framework for determining how best to use precious resources. It should be evident to readers that we perceive inclusive education as ever evolving, achievable in different ways, and the product of sustained commitment and problem solving.

Throughout the book we suggest a goal of "maximizing" the inclusiveness of your school. The reality is that some students need, and deserve, intensive or specialized services that are best delivered through a continuum of services. However, the effort to support a learner in the general education setting must also be maximized, and we are confident that with effective leadership, teams can increase both time and achievement in an inclusive classroom. It is our hope that this book can provide guidance to those with this enormous responsibility—acting as a map for their own running paths.

Acknowledgments

We wish to thank the many colleagues, teachers and team members, parents, and students who have been the real leaders in helping others understand what it means to be inclusive. One benefit of our longevity has been the opportunity to learn from idealists, pragmatists, and motivators, for whom we have deep respect. We wish to thank Catherine Wang for being an exemplar we can learn from and for serving as a sounding board for our ideas for this book. We also wish to thank our acquisitions editor, Rebecca Lazo, for her insight, guidance, and constructive feedback throughout this process, and Steve Plocher, for his thoughtful editing.

Thomas wishes to acknowledge his former colleagues and parents in Grayslake District 46 and Glencoe District 35, who adopted a student-centered approach to serving all learners and who exemplified what it means to be collaborative.

Dennis wishes to thank Carthage College for the sabbatical leave in Spring 2009 to start this work. He also wishes to acknowledge Dr. Toni Van Laarhoven, friend and co-researcher on Project ACCEPT, for her commitment to preparing preservice educators to be strong advocates and effective teachers in inclusive classrooms.

*To my wife, Karen, without whose understanding and support I could not
have attempted, or completed, this project. And to my sons Caleb and Sam—you have
helped me understand the significance of being valued and respected by teachers and classmates.*

—DM

To Jeff, Tim, Joe, and Leroy, who inspired me to start down this road 38 years ago.

—TD

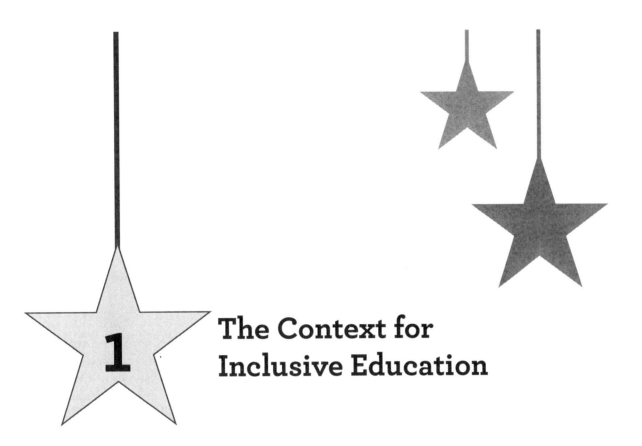

The Context for Inclusive Education

Since the 1980s, general and special educators have experienced a progressive but dramatic evolution of ideology and practice in serving learners with diverse abilities, including those with special needs. Images of the typical and ideal classrooms have evolved as an increasingly diverse population of learners has challenged our assumptions about educational potential and sparked reform in how educational services and supports are structured and evaluated. Professionals in the field of special education have continued to seek and develop effective instructional methods for learners with special needs, while contemplating—and often debating—whether learners are better served within the general education classroom or in special classrooms for all or part of the day. The term *inclusion* has come to represent the practice of educating learners with special needs in the general education classroom. In the 1980s, many in the field viewed this as an abrupt change in direction for a field that was formally created only a decade earlier by the Education for All Handicapped Children Act of 1975 (PL 94-142). The research and debate that ensued since then—and that continue today—have answered many questions about how best to serve learners in an inclusive setting, but also suggested that positive outcomes depend on a confluence of several factors related to the school environment, including expertise of teachers. What is clear is that the success of included learners is not guaranteed or the product of some known formula, but is rather the product of a well-designed and responsive program of inclusive education. All learners deserve effective, inclusive education; leadership is the key to making it happen in every school.

Our purpose in creating this resource for school administrators, teachers, specialists, and parents is to provide a succinct and convenient overview of practices that promote positive outcomes for included learners and encourage ongoing enhancement of your inclusive education program. We use a leadership strategy founded on four areas of practice identified as being essential for effective inclusion:

1

1. Establishing an inclusive school culture

2. Seeking and implementing research-based practices

3. Engaging in schoolwide collaboration

4. Conducting ongoing reflection and evaluation

The need for sustained commitment to inclusive education is greater than ever as schools strive to meet the requirements of the No Child Left Behind Act of 2001 (NCLB; PL 107-110), particularly that of adequate yearly progress, by improving access to the general education curriculum. Balancing emphases on adequate yearly progress and the least restrictive environment for learners with special needs requires leadership at the district, school, and classroom levels.

Research on implementation of inclusive education, coupled with our collective 40 years of experience in inclusive settings, suggests that implementing and sustaining effective inclusion practices requires a schoolwide commitment and the establishment of structures and practices that are integrated into the overall mission of the school—not just viewed as a special project driven by the vision and energy of select individuals. All too often, schools have "geared up" for inclusion, only to have their focus and enthusiasm diminished as a result of staff turnover, school initiatives that compete for staff attention and resources (e.g., making adequate yearly progress), lingering resistance and attitudinal barriers, or the realities of supporting a learner with particularly challenging needs. Thus, although the general education setting has always existed as one option along a continuum of special education services, the extent to which educational teams perceive it as the least restrictive environment is too often influenced by what is available, not what is necessary.

PERSPECTIVE ON INCLUSIVE EDUCATION

Inclusion and *inclusive education* are terms that have become part of the vernacular of education, although interpretations vary among users. We define *inclusive education* as a comprehensive approach to school functioning that is based on the following core values and assumptions and specific practices:

1. Critical values and assumptions:
   - All learners are afforded the same respect and dignity as members of the school community.
   - All learners are capable of growing and achieving academically and socially.
   - All learners benefit from the presence of diversity among classmates.

2. Critical schoolwide practices:
   - School personnel accept shared ownership for education of all learners.
   - Schoolwide policies and practices are designed for the benefit of all learners.
   - The administration and teachers expect and prepare for diversity among learners.

3. Critical classwide practices:
   - Teachers respect individual differences among classmates and expect all to meet challenging goals and expectations.

- Teachers demonstrate respect for all learners in their daily interactions and promote positive relationships among classmates.
- Grouping of learners is time limited, flexible, and designed to promote blending of abilities; when used to deliver supplemental instruction or extra support, it is based on need and not on a label.

4. Implementation of special education services:
   - General and special education personnel share responsibility for education of learners with special needs.
   - The overarching goal in designing, implementing, and monitoring services is to maximize participation and achievement in the general education setting and curriculum.
   - Successful inclusion involves both physical integration and an effective program of individualized instruction, accommodations, and supports—not simply placement in a general education classroom.

Inclusive education is not simply the placement of learners in a general education classroom, which without an effective program of support can lead to negative outcomes and a default assumption that special classrooms or pull-out services are more appropriate.

Important Terms

Terms that we use throughout this book are defined as follows:

- *Learners with special needs* refers primarily to those students who are at risk or eligible for special education services because of the presence of a disability, but may also include English language learners or students from impoverished environments. Where appropriate, we refer specifically to learners receiving special education services.
- *Educational teams* refers to the administrators (e.g., principal, assistant principal, curriculum director), classroom teachers (e.g., general educator, special educator), and specialists (e.g., psychologist, social worker, counselor, speech therapist, occupational therapist, physical therapist) who support learners with special needs.
- *IEP teams* refers to the principal, classroom teachers, specialists, parents, and students who develop, implement, and monitor the individualized education program (IEP) for learners who receive special education services.
- *Inclusive education* refers to the collection of school practices that are intended to maximize the success of all learners in the general education curriculum and culture. An inclusive education program involves schoolwide and classwide practices, as well as services and supports for individual groups of learners with specific needs.
- *General education (educator)* is used throughout the text rather than the common alternative of *regular education (educator),* except in quotations, reprinted figures, or legal language.

THE CONTEXT FOR INCLUSIVE EDUCATION

Inclusive education for learners receiving special education services has evolved since the 1980s within a context of research and policy making that has informed current practice. Leaders should be familiar with the legal, philosophical, and empirical foundations that have shaped the present status of inclusive practices.

Table 1.1. Percentage of the day that students with disabilities (ages 6–21 years) spent in the general education classroom in the 2003–2004 school year

Disability	80% or more of the day	79%–40% of the day	Less than 40% of the day	Not in a general education school
Specific learning disability	48.8	37.3	13.0	0.9
Speech or language impairment	88.2	6.8	4.6	0.4
Intellectual disability	11.7	30.2	51.8	6.3
Emotional disturbance	30.3	22.6	30.2	16.9
Multiple disabilities	12.1	17.2	45.8	24.9
Hearing impairment	44.9	19.2	22.2	13.7
Orthopedic impairment	46.7	20.9	26.2	6.2
Other health impairment	51.1	30.5	15.0	3.5
Visual impairment	54.6	16.9	15.6	12.8
Autism	26.8	17.7	43.9	11.6
Deaf-blindness	22.2	13.9	33.6	30.3
Traumatic brain injury	34.6	29.9	27.1	8.4
Developmental delay	51.2	28.2	18.6	2.0
All disabilities	49.9	27.7	18.5	3.9

Source: U.S. Department of Education (2007).
Note: Percentages rounded to nearest tenths place.

The Status of Physical Inclusion

Table 1.1 depicts where learners are receiving special education services, and Table 1.2 depicts placement data for 1995 to 2005. Together, these data suggest that 1) an overwhelming percentage of learners across all disability types continue to receive some services outside the general education classroom; and 2) the percentage of time spent in the general education classrooms increased only modestly between 1995 and 2005 despite considerable nationwide efforts to increase inclusive placements. What cannot be ascertained from the data are the reasons why IEP teams have not pinpointed the general education classroom as the least restrictive environment for more learners. Related research (e.g., Downing, Eichinger, & Williams, 1997; Scruggs & Mastropieri, 1996) and our experience suggest that placement in the general education classroom often is not prioritized because of perceptions that the general education staff lack the specialized training to serve diverse learners or that the school simply lacks the adequate resources to support included learners. Such concerns are heightened by increased focus on meeting adequate yearly progress, especially when schools fail to establish an overarching mission that embodies high achievement in the general education curriculum and culture for all learners.

Legal Interpretations of the Least Restrictive Environment

From its inception, the law guaranteeing special education services has required that learners be educated in the least restrictive environment. According to the Individuals with Disabilities Education Improvement Act (IDEA) of 2004 (PL 108-446), a least restrictive environment is determined on a case-by-case basis to ensure that each student's special needs are met, while allowing that student the maximum possible exposure to students without disabilities as well as the general education curriculum. A major determinant of the least restrictive environment is the extent to which a learner can make satisfactory progress and be successful. Two court cases have cited factors that influence determination of the least restrictive environment. In *Oberti v. Board of Education of the Borough of Clementon School District*

Table 1.2. Percentage of the day that students with disabilities (ages 6–21 years) spent in the general education classroom in the decade 1995–2005

Year	80% or more of the day	79%–40% of the day	Less than 40% of the day	Not in a general education school
1995–1996	45.3	28.7	21.6	4.4
1996–1997	45.8	28.5	21.4	4.3
1997–1998	46.4	29.0	20.4	4.1
1998–1999	46.1	29.8	20.1	4.1
1999–2000	46.0	29.7	20.3	4.1
2000–2001	46.5	29.8	19.5	4.2
2001–2002	48.4	28.3	19.2	4.0
2002–2003	48.2	28.7	19.0	4.0
2003–2004	49.9	27.7	18.5	3.9
2004–2005	51.9	26.5	17.6	4.0
2005–2006	54.2	25.1	16.7	4.1

Source: National Center for Education Statistics (2007).
Note: Percentages rounded to nearest tenths place.

(1993), the court found that 1) schools must consider whether a child can progress satisfactorily in the general education classroom with the use of supplemental aids and services, and 2) if placement outside the general education classroom is deemed necessary for part of the day, an attempt must be made to maximize time spent in the general education classroom. In another case addressing the least restrictive environment (*Sacramento City Unified School District Board of Education v. Rachel H.,* 1994), a California circuit court found that schools must consider four factors when determining if the general education classroom is the least restrictive environment: 1) the perceived educational benefits of placement in the general education classroom; 2) the perceived nonacademic benefits of placement in the general education classroom; 3) the impact of the student's presence on the rest of the class; and 4) the cost of placement in the general education classroom (Osborne & Russo, 2006). Among the reasons IEP teams may determine the need for placement outside the classroom are lack of adequate progress; excessive costs to support the learner; the requirement for more specialized services, programs, or environments; and disruption to the education of the other students (Osborne & Russo, 2006).

What is obvious in the legal interpretations of the least restrictive environment is that the ability of the learner to be successful in the general education classroom is the most important factor. In schools that value inclusiveness, teams seek to maximize the potential for success in the general education classroom and avoid assumptions that a more restrictive placement is necessary because of the nature of disability. In essence, the philosophy should be that learners must earn their way into a more restrictive placement—not the alternative of having to meet certain expectations to "earn" an inclusive classroom.

NCLB, IDEA, and Inclusive Education

NCLB of 2001 and IDEA of 2004 share a focus on high expectations for all learners, including those with special needs, with consequences for schools who fail to make adequate yearly progress. To many, the provisions of the two acts are contradictory in that NCLB seeks to standardize the curriculum and assessment procedures, whereas the IDEA continues to emphasize an IEP. Others have argued that both acts seek to ensure high-quality instruction and accountability measures for learners with special needs and should therefore provide the impetus for important changes in the way special education services are delivered (Cole, 2006; Ratcliffe & Willard, 2006).

Table 1.3. Similarities and differences between the No Child Left Behind Act of 2001 (PL 107-110) and the Individuals with Disabilities Education Improvement Act of 2004 (PL 108-446)

	No Child Left Behind Act	Individuals with Disabilities Education Improvement Act
Similar provisions		
Participation in accountability assessments	Full participation in grade-level assessments; accommodations and alternate assessments as allowed under the Individuals with Disabilities Education Improvement Act	Similar language, but does not specify "grade-level" assessments
Qualified personnel	"Highly qualified" personnel determined by evidence of content area expertise	"Qualified" personnel as evidenced by certification or licensing in areas being taught
Contrasting provisions		
Curricular emphasis	Emphasis on core academic areas tested: reading and mathematics	Emphasis on improving academic, social, and functional/life skills
Use of accommodations	Testing accommodations regulated by state	Individualized education program teams determine how and when accommodations should be implemented based on learner's needs.

Sources: Cole (2006); Ratcliffe & Willard (2006).

Both acts have drawn praise and criticism. Although neither act speaks explicitly about inclusive education, their emphasis on performance in the general curriculum and requirements that all learners achieve adequate yearly progress may have unintended effects on inclusive practices. School leaders must be sensitive to the similarities and contradictions of the two acts and understand how initiatives intended to improve student achievement can undermine the mission of inclusive education. Table 1.3 presents a synopsis of shared and contrasting provisions for NCLB and IDEA. The most common area for tension is in the curricular emphases, for which the IDEA upholds the historical view that learners should be instructed at their level of achievement and that social/functional skills share priority with those in academic areas.

Table 1.4 presents strategies that promote progress toward inclusive education and adequate yearly progress. The common thread for all of the positive approaches is the pursuit of high achievement for all learners in the general education curriculum and setting. With that goal in mind, strategies that lead to separation and remediation seem obviously counterproductive. In Chapter 5, we discuss how increasing access to challenging courses is a characteristic of exemplary high schools for high achievement and inclusiveness.

Chapter 6 includes a guide for creating a snapshot of where your students are being served, trends in placement and program decisions, and achievement of those with special needs (see Tool 6.1). Establishing a clear picture of where you are is the first step in determining goals for sustaining and increasing effective practices.

HISTORICAL CONTEXT: RESEARCH AND DISCOURSE ON INCLUSION

Inclusive education both envelops and surpasses traditional notions of inclusion of learners with special needs. Nonetheless, familiarity with the national discourse regarding inclusion is vital for school leaders, as many of those issues resonate today in the attitudes and perceptions of school personnel and parents. Indeed, the historical discussion regarding inclusion symbol-

Table 1.4.   Strategies that support and undermine progress toward adequate yearly progress and inclusive education

Supportive strategies	Undermining strategies
Establish a mission and vision that encompass both success in the general education setting and meeting adequate yearly progress as examples of high standards for all learners. Help staff "connect the dots" between the overall quality of your inclusive education program and scores on high-stakes assessments.	Focus on improving test scores through a series of fragmented initiatives that are carried out in isolation and that are not related to the quality of the overall inclusive education program. Implement "remediation" for those who did not meet standards.
Ensure that all learners are working in a curriculum that is aligned with the state learning standards and indicators where available.	Increase instructional time on reading and math for learners who did not meet standards. Narrow the existing curriculum by eliminating course options or "doubling up" on language arts or math periods or classes.
Implement progress monitoring for all learners as a means for detecting slow progress and determining the need to adjust instruction. Use response-to-intervention procedures as part of overarching goal of schoolwide accountability.	Rely on a "teach and hope" approach in which curricular or instructional changes made in response to low test scores remain intact until the following set of scores are received. Learners are placed in remedial instruction for the entire year.
Provide teachers with professional development and resources (e.g., materials) necessary to instruct learners with diverse needs in inclusive classrooms. Professional development is timely and designed to meet the most pressing needs as identified by teachers.	Charge teachers with improving student achievement by working harder and increasing their expectations for learners. Provide "one-shot" trainings with no ongoing support or provide different professional development for general and special educators.

ized the complex set of beliefs and practices that leaders must consider in designing inclusive education that is successful in the eyes of the school administration, teachers, parents, and learners. This section provides a concise summary of the research and debate on inclusion that continue to inform opinions and practices today.

Although the potential benefits and limitations of educating learners with special needs with their peers had been discussed in the professional literature in previous decades, advocacy for such practice increased significantly in the 1980s. In a highly cited work, Will (1986) asserted that special classroom and pull-out services had not proven effective in the decade following the genesis of the field of special education with the Education for All Handicapped Children Act of 1975 and that reform involving the merging of special and general education services would better serve all learners. Often termed the *Regular Education Initiative,* this proposal sparked national debate centered on multiple themes, including legal, philosophical, and empirical bases for inclusion in the general education classroom. In this context, the term *inclusion* emerged to describe the practice of educating learners with exceptionalities in the general education setting, in contrast to the historical practice of mainstreaming learners for part of their day. Full-time placement and support in the general education classroom with no pull-out services became known as *full inclusion;* this quickly became the topic of much debate among advocates, researchers, and practitioners (Kavale & Forness, 2000).

For advocates in the years prior to the Education for All Handicapped Children Act of 1975, the basis for inclusion was found in the civil rights legislation—specifically the landmark case of *Brown v. Board of Education* (1954), which established that separate services are inherently unequal (Stainback & Smith, 2005). Segregated settings—particularly those for individuals with intellectual disabilities—came under scrutiny as advocates successfully argued that individuals with disabilities possessed the right to be served in environments with their peers. For some, inclusion remains a matter of civil rights, although this perspective is controversial and has been largely displaced by a focus on how we should establish the least restrictive environment, as required for all learners receiving special education services.

In the period from 1986 to 2000, the field of special education engaged in considerable discourse regarding inclusionary practices. Participants included academic researchers, practitioners, advocates, and parents, who were often characterized as "pro-inclusion" or "anti-inclusion." In reality, such polarizing descriptors are not only imprecise but distract from the legitimate issues under discussion. One area of discussion and research was the preparedness of general education to serve learners with special needs, given that the intent of special education was to serve learners who historically had not been successful in the general education setting. Early research focused on general educators' attitudes and preparedness to instruct and support learners with special needs (e.g., Baker & Zigmond, 1995; Schumm & Vaughn, 1995; Scruggs & Mastropieri, 1996); the impact of included learners on the academic achievement (e.g., Hollowood, Salisbury, Rainforth, & Palombaro, 1994; Sharpe, York, & Knight, 1994) and social interactions (e.g., Capper & Pickett, 1994; Helmstetter, Peck, & Giangreco, 1994) of their general education peers; learner preferences for inclusion versus pull-out (e.g. Padeliadu & Zigmond, 1996; Reid & Button, 1995); and the success of learners in inclusive or pull-out settings, which we summarize later in this section. In general, the early research suggested positive or neutral effects of inclusion on the achievement of both learners with special needs and their peers. Research on the readiness of general educators suggested concerns regarding their ability to provide accommodations and deliver specialized, individualized instruction.

As the body of research on inclusion began to build, some critics argued that such research was not necessary or useful because the case for inclusion was based on the learner's right to be educated with his or her peers; it therefore should not be a research-based decision. Furthermore, research suggesting that general education was not prepared to serve all learners might be cited as a barrier to inclusion, whereas an alternative view might hold that the presence of included learners would facilitate necessary changes in philosophy or practice. The debate extended beyond the question of usefulness to matters of epistemology and the assumptions underlying traditional research methods in education (e.g., Danforth & Rhodes, 1997; Kavale & Mostert, 2003).

Numerous research studies have investigated the performance of learners with exceptionalities in the general education classroom, a pull-out placement, or a combination of both arrangements. Several studies have reported positive academic achievement (Baker, Wang, & Walberg, 1995; Banerji & Dailey, 1995; Fuchs, Fuchs, & Fernstrom, 1993; Waldron & McLeskey, 1998) and social interactions as outcomes for learners with significant disabilities (Fryxell & Kennedy, 1995; McDonnell et al., 2003) and mild disabilities (Banerji & Dailey, 1995; Vaughn, Elbaum, Schumm, & Hughes, 1998). Freeman (2000) reviewed 36 studies on the academic achievement and social outcomes for included learners with intellectual disabilities and found evidence of academic achievement gains and increased social competence, but no effect on social acceptance by peers. A more recent study investigated the effect of an inclusive setting incorporating specified practices and multiple measures of academic achievement, including "high-stakes" tests. Rea, McLaughlin, and Walther-Thomas (2002) compared the performance of eighth-grade students with learning disabilities in an inclusive or a pull-out model of special education services. The inclusive model included team teaching and collaborative planning; all special education services, including supplementary instruction, were provided in the general education classroom. Furthermore, included learners had more objectives addressing the academic curriculum in their IEPs, had more accommodations for classroom instruction and assessment, and received more than twice the minutes of special education services per week as their counterparts in the pull-out model. A comparison of the performance of the two groups revealed that those in the inclusive setting achieved significantly higher report card grades in language arts, math, science, and social studies. Performance on a state proficiency test indicated roughly equivalent performances, whereas on the Iowa Test of Basic Skills the included learners scored higher in language arts and math. Comparisons on nonacademic measures revealed no difference in suspensions for the two groups and higher attendance for the included learners. The study's authors conclude that schools can design and implement inclusive education that includes multiple features, including shared responsibility of all teachers and administrators.

Although ample evidence suggests academic and social advantages to use of the inclusive setting, research has suggested that some included learners may require more intense supports than those currently provided in their inclusive classrooms (e.g., Carlberg & Kavale, 1980; Holloway, 2001). Supporting learners with emotional and behavior disabilities may be particularly challenging given their need for highly individualized IEPs and classroom supports. For this reason, a more cautious approach has been taken to including learners with serious emotional and behavioral concerns (Simpson, 2004). For some, the challenge of trying to establish a common understanding of inclusion, coupled with the research findings suggesting that learner performance may not be influenced as much by physical placement as what happens in their classrooms (e.g., Fore, Hagan-Burke, Burke, Boon, & Smith, 2008), implies that research attention should be shifted to *how* rather than just *where* (Zigmond, 2003). The suggestion to expand or evolve the focus of research beyond placement is consistent with our conceptualization of inclusive education as a commitment to both the general education setting and an effective educational program.

The purpose of this concise overview of past research and discourse is to inform or refresh readers' understanding of the concepts and issues that have been so vigorously investigated and debated since the 1980s. Interpreting such research is difficult because the characteristics of learners and the ways in which inclusive and pull-out programs are designed and delivered vary from school to school. Inclusion does not represent a well-defined independent variable that can be tested repeatedly across different settings to verify its impact (e.g., Fuchs & Fuchs, 1994; Simpson, 2004). Although the historical debate regarding inclusion has been both passionate and polarizing, the underlying goal has remained to provide the highest quality educational experience for learners with special needs. Leaders of inclusive education should expect to encounter some parents and school personnel who perceive inclusion as a basic right for all learners, whereas others may view the general education classroom as a preferred or viable option along a continuum, with placement decisions based on the learner's actual experience and achievement in school. Table 1.5 provides a synopsis of the research and discourse for those who are forming their own perspective on inclusive education or who must explain the foundation for current practices to colleagues or parents.

LEADERSHIP AND THE QUEST FOR INCLUSIVE EDUCATION

Clearly, leadership is necessary if we are to increase the number of learners receiving services in the general education classroom, facilitate achievement on both individual goals and the general education curriculum, and ensure that learners with special needs achieve full participation and benefit from their school experience.

Our purpose in creating this resource is to promote strategic leadership among school administrators, teachers, and specialists in the pursuit of effective and sustained practices. We chose the term *strategic leadership* to describe a systematic approach to leadership that targets specific areas of practice and that involves the coordinated efforts of many. In our view, leadership is being provided in all schools, often by many different individuals and often with

Table 1.5. Synopsis of historical research and discourse on inclusive practices

1. An education with same-age peers in the general education setting is the ideal for all learners. Special education services should focus on maximizing access to, and success in, that setting.

2. Teams should consider academic achievement, social benefits, and learner perceptions when determining how (or whether) satisfactory progress can be made in the general education setting. No single measure is adequate for determining whether the general education classroom is indeed the least restrictive environment.

3. An ample body of research suggests that learners with special needs can be as (or more) successful in an inclusive placement than in a special class or pull-out model. The bulk of supportive research has been conducted with learners with learning and intellectual disabilities, with less focus on those with emotional and behavioral disabilities. Outcome studies have used various definitions and designs for inclusion, and some findings suggest that the benefits of inclusion are derived from the combination of placement and effective services—not either implemented alone.

4. General educators are generally supportive of serving included learners—assuming they receive adequate professional development and ongoing support. Similarly, learners with special needs prefer to learn in the general classroom as long as they receive adequate support for challenging work—assuming that the teacher has created a classroom environment that promotes respect for individual differences. When these conditions are not met, both teachers and learners are more likely to perceive services delivered outside the classroom as better suited to the learner's needs.

impressive results. However, leadership in inclusive education often consists of one-time initiatives chosen to address a specific issue, flurries of professional development without ongoing support, projects spearheaded by the personal experiences and interests of one or a few individuals, or failure to take advantage of existing expertise already on board.

To reiterate, inclusive education is a dynamic, ever-evolving approach that requires ongoing reflection and continuous enhancement. Strategic leadership toward such goals must be systematic, sustainable, participatory, and adaptable. This resource is intended to serve as a guide toward strategic leadership in inclusive education.

ELEMENTS OF LEADERSHIP FOR INCLUSIVE EDUCATION

In inclusive education, leaders seek to promote practices that maximize access to (and success in) the general education classroom, curriculum, and culture. Leadership may be evidenced in creating new policies, forming new structures, learning new strategies, consistently monitoring effective practices, or advocating for an included learner.

Who Should Lead?

All members of the educational team should consider themselves to have potential and responsibility for leadership. Although specific duties may reside with administrators or teachers, the responsibility for constantly looking for ways to enhance inclusive practices should be distributed among all team members. Consequently, those traditionally viewed as having the power to make decisions (typically the special education administrator and the principal) must recognize the need for distributed responsibility and "role release" among team members.

How Should They Lead?

Leadership may involve schoolwide practices (e.g., creating a new mission statement emphasizing inclusiveness), classwide practices (e.g., implementing differentiation in assessments used for grading), or services and support for individual learners (e.g., teach pivotal social skills to enhance interactions on the playground). Thus, leadership is evidenced in highly visible actions such as policy development, as well as in more subtle behaviors, such as actively engaging in problem solving to improve a learner's writing ability. For schools to deliver the best services possible, leadership must be viewed as an ongoing endeavor. Fortunately, specific areas of practice have emerged as critical to creating and maintaining inclusive education.

WRAPPING UP AND LOOKING AHEAD

Research has indicated numerous threats to the sustainability of inclusive education, including changes in administrators, staff turnover, shifts in priorities and allocation of resources, control concentrated in just top administrators, and lingering perceptions of special education as a separate system (Mamlin, 1999; Sindelar, Shearer, Yendol-Hoppey, & Liebert, 2006). To minimize the impact of these threats, leaders must approach their program as a dynamic, ever-evolving entity that requires consistent evaluation and refining. The remainder of this book addresses ideas, concepts, and practices related to inclusive education that are especially relevant for school leaders. This book is not intended as a methods book in classroom strategies; several of these are already available. Rather, we attempt to highlight what needs to be done to establish an environment in which teachers can and do use recommended instructional strategies. Our focus on policies, structures, and frameworks takes shape in Chapter 2, which describes a leadership strategy that guides activities in areas that are critical to effective inclusive education.

RECOMMENDED RESOURCES

Families and Advocates Partnership for Education (http://www.fape.org)

Kavale, K.A., & Forness, S.R. (2000). History, rhetoric, and reality: Analysis of the inclusion debate. *Remedial and Special Education, 21*(2), 279–296.

Kids Together (http://www.kidstogether.org)

Office of Special Education and Rehabilitative Services (http://www.ed.gov/about/office/list/osep/index.html)

PBS Parents Inclusive Education Site (http://www.pbs.org/parents/inclusivecommunities/inclusive_education.html)

Stainback, S.B., & Smith, J. (2005). Inclusive education: Historical perspectives. In R.A. Villa & J.S. Thousand (Eds.), *Creating an inclusive school* (2nd ed.). Alexandria, VA: Association for Supervision and Curriculum Development.

Wrightslaw (http://www.wrightslaw.com)

Zigmond, N. (2003). Where should students with disabilities receive special education services? Is one place better than another? *Journal of Special Education, 37*(1), 93–199.

REFERENCES

Baker, E., Wang, M., & Walberg, H. (1995). The effects of inclusion on learning. *Educational Leadership, 52*(4), 33–34.

Baker, J.M., & Zigmond, N. (1995). The meaning and practice of inclusion of students with learning disabilities. Themes and implications for the five cases. *Journal of Special Education, 29*(2), 163–180.

Banerji, M., & Dailey, R.A. (1995). A study of the effects of an inclusion model on students with specific learning disabilities. *Journal of Learning Disabilities, 28*(4), 511–523.

Brown v. Board of Education, Topeka, 347 U.S. 483 (1954).

Capper, C.A., & Pickett, R.S. (1994). The relationship between school structure and culture and student views of diversity in inclusive education. *The Special Education Leadership Review, 2,* 102–122.

Carlberg, C., & Kavale, K. (1980). The efficacy of special versus general education class placement for exceptional children: A meta-analysis. *Journal of Special Education, 14*(3), 295–309.

Cole, C. (2006). Closing the achievement gap series: Part III—What is the impact of NCLB on the inclusion of students with disabilities? *Education Policy Brief, 4*(11), 1–12.

Danforth, S., & Rhodes, W.C. (1997). Deconstructing disability: A philosophy for inclusion. *Remedial and Special Education, 18,* 357–366.

Downing, J.E., Eichinger, J., & Williams, L.J. (1997). Inclusive education for students with severe disabilities: Comparative views of principals and educators of different levels of implementation. *Remedial and Special Education, 18,* 133–142.

Education for All Handicapped Children Act of 1975, PL 94-142, 20 U.S.C. §§ 3801 *et seq.*

Fore, C., Hagan-Burke, S., Burke, M., Boon, R.T., & Smith, S. (2008). Academic achievement and class placement in high school: Do students with learning disabilities achieve more in one class placement than another? *Education and Treatment of Children, 31*(1), 55–72.

Freeman, S. (2000). Academic and social attainments of children with mental retardation in general education and special education settings. *Remedial and Special Education, 21*(1), 3–11.

Fryxell, D., & Kennedy, C. (1995). Placement along the curriculum of services and its impact on students' social relationships. *Journal of the Association for Persons with Severe Handicaps, 20*(2), 259–269.

Fuchs, D., & Fuchs, L.S. (1994). Inclusive schools movement and the radicalization of special education. *Exceptional Children, 60*(3), 294–309.

Fuchs, D., Fuchs, L., & Fernstrom, P. (1993). A conservative approach to special education reform: Mainstreaming through transenvironmental programming and curriculum-based measurement. *American Educational Research Journal, 30,* 149–177.

Helmstetter, E., Peck, C.A., & Giangreco, M.F. (1994). Outcomes of interactions with peers with moderate or severe disabilities: A statewide survey of high school students. *Journal of the Association for Persons with Severe Handicaps, 19,* 263–276.

Holloway, J.H. (2001). Inclusion and students with learning disabilities. *Educational Leadership, 58*(1), 86–87.

Hollowood, J.M., Salisbury, C.L., Rainforth, B., & Palombaro, M.M. (1994). Use of instructional time in classrooms serving students with and without severe disabilities. *Exceptional Children, 61*(2), 242–253.

Individuals with Disabilities Education Improvement Act of 2004, PL 108-446, 20 U.S.C. §§ 1400 *et seq.*

Kavale, K.A., & Forness, S.R. (2000). History, rhetoric, and reality: Analysis of the inclusion debate. *Remedial and Special Education, 21*(2), 279–296.

Kavale, K.A., & Mostert, M.P. (2003). River of ideology, islands of evidence. *Exceptionality, 11*(4), 191–208.

Mamlin, N. (1999). Despite best intentions: When inclusion fails. *Journal of Special Education, 33*(1), 36–49.

McDonnell, J., Thorson, N., Disher, S., Mathot-Buckner, C., Mendel, J., & Ray, L. (2003). The achievement of students with developmental disabilities and their peers without disabilities in inclusive settings: An exploratory study. *Education and Treatment of Children, 26*(2), 224–236.

National Center for Education Statistics (2007). *The Condition of education 2007: Inclusion of students with disabilities in general classrooms.* Washington, DC: Institute of Education Sciences of the U.S. Department of Education.

No Child Left Behind Act of 2001, PL 107-110, 115 Stat. 1425, 20 U.S.C §§ 6301 *et seq.*

Oberti v. Board of Education of the Borough of Clementon School District, 995 F.2d 1204 (3d Cir. 1993).

Osborne, A.G., & Russo, C.J. (2006). *Special education and the law: A guide for practitioners* (2nd ed.). Thousand Oaks, CA: Corwin.

Padeliadu, S., & Zigmond, N. (1996). Perspectives of students with learning disabilities about special education placement. *Learning Disabilities Research and Practice, 11*(1), 15–23.

Ratcliffe, K.G., & Willard, D.J. (2006). NCLB and IDEA: Perspectives from the field. *Focus on Exceptional Children, 39*(3), 1–14.

Rea, P.J., McLaughlin, V.L., & Walther-Thomas, C. (2002). Outcomes for students with learning disabilities in inclusive and pullout programs. *Exceptional Children, 68*(2), 203–227.

Reid, D.K. & Button, L.J. (1995). Anna's story: Narratives of personal experience about being labeled learning disabled. *Journal of Learning Disabilities, 28*(4), 602–614.

Sacramento City Unified School District Board of Education v. Rachel H., 14 F.3d 1398 (9th Cir. 1994), *cert. denied,* 512 U.S. 1207 (1994).

Schumm, J.S., & Vaughn, S. (1995). Getting ready for inclusion. Is the stage set? *Learning Disability Research and Practice, 10*(1), 169–179.

Scruggs, T.E., & Mastropieri, M.A. (1996). Teacher perceptions of mainstreaming and inclusion, 1958–1995: A research synthesis. *Exceptional Children, 63*(1), 59–74.

Sharpe, M.N., York, J.L., & Knight, J. (1994). Effects of inclusion on the academic performance of classmates without disabilities. *Remedial and Special Education, 15*(2), 281–287.

Simpson, R.L. (2004). Inclusion of students with behavior disorders in general education settings: Research and measurement issues. *Behavioral Disorders, 30*(1), 19–31.

Sindelar, P.T., Shearer, D.K., Yendol-Hoppey, D., & Liebert, T.W. (2006). The sustainability of inclusive school reform. *Exceptional Children, 72*(3), 317–331.

Stainback, S.B., & Smith, J. (2005). Inclusive education: Historical perspectives. In R.A. Villa & J.S. Thousand (Eds.), *Creating an inclusive school* (2nd ed.). Alexandria, VA: Association for Supervision and Curriculum Development.

U.S. Department of Education (2007). *Twenty-seventh annual report to Congress on the implementation of the Individuals with Disabilities Education Act* (vol. I, p. 44). Washington, DC.

Vaughn, S., Elbaum, B.E., Schumm, J.S., & Hughes, M.T. (1998). Social outcomes for students with and without learning disabilities in inclusive classrooms. *Journal of Learning Disabilities, 31*(5), 428–436.

Waldron, N.L., & McLeskey, J. (1998). The effects of an inclusive school program on students with mild and severe learning disabilities. *Exceptional Children, 64*(3), 395–405.

Will, M.C. (1986). Educating children with learning problems—A shared responsibility. *Exceptional Children, 52*(5), 411–416.

Zigmond, N. (2003). Where should students with disabilities receive special education services? Is one place better than another? *Journal of Special Education, 37*(1), 93–199.

2   The STAR Leadership Strategy

Inclusive education is an ever-evolving initiative that requires a coordinated set of practices carried out by administrators, teachers, and specialists. Research on inclusive education (Cushing, Carter, Clark, Wallis, & Kennedy, 2009; Gersten & Dimino, 2001; Murawski & Dieker, 2004; Thousand & Villa, 2005) suggests that schools are successful when they use the following four practices of the STAR leadership strategy:

1. *Setting the tone:* Establishing a schoolwide culture based on equality, democracy, and valuing of differences

2. *Translating research into practice:* Seeking out and using effective practices in blended classrooms

3. *Arranging for collaboration:* Encouraging and enabling collaboration between professionals

4. *Reflecting on processes and outcomes:* Evaluating successes and seeking to remedy limitations

The STAR leadership strategy is a tool for guiding teams in planning, implementing, and evaluating activities in each of the four critical areas of practice (see Table 2.1). A multicomponent strategy allows schools to identify their strengths and needs, as well as focus energy and resources in areas of greatest need. The flexibility of a strategy allows teams to address many of the threats to inclusive efforts, particularly the concentration of power with just a few individuals. This chapter describes how each of four areas of practice contribute to an inclusive outcome and what types of leadership activities are required. The chapter concludes with a case study describing implementation of the STAR leadership strategy in a representative school district.

STAR ORGANIZER

Table 2.1.

FOUR LEADERSHIP AREAS IN THE STAR STRATEGY

AREA	SAMPLE ACTIVITIES	IMPORTANCE
Setting the tone	• Create mission/vision statements that establish inclusiveness as a standard for all school practices. • Adopt policies and procedures that are designed to serve and benefit all learners. • Acknowledge the successes of community members who exemplify mission of inclusiveness.	The school's culture must be founded on a set of core values and beliefs that inform all policies, practices, and decisions if inclusive education is to be achieved. Community members should recognize when their actions are (or are not) consistent with the values and beliefs of the larger school culture. Inclusive practices will not be valued or sustained if the school has not adopted a core set of values and beliefs into its mission or vision.
 *Translating research into practice*	• Identify sources for information and establish a routine for accessing sources on a regular basis. • Create structures for discussion of new ideas and practices among team members and development of a plan for implementation. • Develop professional development opportunities that promote the use of new practices with fidelity.	Educational teams must constantly update their knowledge of methods and strategies for serving included learners. Research on how to instruct, support, and assess learners in blended classrooms is constantly in progress, but is underused in many classrooms. Research has provided the why for inclusive education, but without knowledge of how many teachers will not be successful.

SETTING THE TONE

The phrase *setting the tone* describes how an inclusive school culture is shaped and sustained by its community members. Thousand and Villa (2005, p. 59) used the term *visioning* to describe the articulation of the critical values and beliefs that underlie inclusive education—namely that all children can learn, all children have the right to be educated with their peers, and schools are responsible for the success of all learners. Setting the tone is the responsibility of

AREA	SAMPLE ACTIVITIES	IMPORTANCE
Arranging for collaboration	• Communicate mission and goals to all stakeholders. • Include special and general educators on all decision-making committees for the school. • Create a schedule that provides shared planning time and makes coteaching feasible.	Research has identified collaborative problem solving, planning, and teaching as critical features of effective inclusive education. Furthermore, collaboration among stakeholders requires creation of structures and expectations, not treatment as an ideal that only some teams will achieve.
 **Reflecting on processes and outcomes**	• Solicit feedback from learners and their families on what is working and where improvement is needed. • Analyze data that reflect academic achievement, progress on individual goals, and participation in the general school community and culture. • Solicit feedback from team members on the effectiveness of the way inclusive education is delivered and suggestions for how it might be improved.	Effective inclusive education involves a complex set of activities and processes; it should never be considered a "finished" product. Practitioners must reflect on practices that work for their students; data should be collected and analyzed on a regular basis.

the whole school community, including the school board, school administration, teachers, specialists, students, and families. Researchers have identified the following as beliefs that undergird an inclusive school culture (Capper & Frattura, 2009; Kennedy & Fisher, 2001; Thousand & Villa, 2005):

• Every learner has the potential to learn, and each deserves the opportunity to fulfill his or her potential.

Table 2.2.   General strategies for setting the tone for inclusive education

Who?	• Form a schoolwide/communitywide advisory committee to craft the mission and vision statements.
	• Ensure that the mission is understood and embraced by the entire community, including the school board, school personnel, students, and families.
	• Model inclusiveness by including a variety of people with different experiences and viewpoints.
What?	• Create a mission statement that includes values and beliefs that will serve to guide schoolwide decision making.
	• Articulate a vision for the school that describes what inclusive education looks like, which can lead to developing benchmarks for monitoring progress.
	• Approach inclusive education as a dynamic, ever-evolving endeavor for which continuous monitoring and implementation of new practices should be viewed as positive growth, not as consequences for poor performance.
How?	• Acknowledge and celebrate positive examples of inclusiveness; highlight actions that exemplify your mission and vision statements.
	• Presume diversity in all classrooms when making decisions regarding the curriculum, discipline, and staffing.
	• Ensure that all staff model high regard for all learners in their words and actions.
	• Ensure that job descriptions and evaluation tools for educational team members reflect shared accountability for all learners, including those with special needs.

- Diversity among learners should be expected and celebrated, as being part of a diverse learning community holds benefits for everyone.
- The school community shares responsibility for the academic and social success of all of its learners.

Issues of fairness arise in all classrooms. Inclusive school communities define fairness as learners receiving what they need to be successful—not as providing the same for everyone, regardless of needs (Welch, 2000). Teachers, peers, and parents understand and appreciate that some learners receive individualized support based on their needs and that such treatment is available to all students based on their needs. Practices that embody an inclusive philosophy address the needs and benefits of all learners, not just a subgroup. Consistency is an important feature of an inclusive school culture. Learners with special needs should expect that rules and expectations will be the same throughout the school day and across their classrooms and teachers (Dieker, 2007). In many schools, educational teams still rely on the method of matching learners with teachers who are perceived as willing to provide supports and who send the message that those with special needs are valued members of the class.

Table 2.2 presents general strategies for setting the tone for inclusive education. Chapter 3 discusses ways in which general education administrators can exert leadership in this area. Later, Chapter 6 provides a tool for developing an inclusive vision statement, which is the first step in setting the tone.

TRANSLATING RESEARCH INTO PRACTICE

As discussed previously, the question of *whether* to pursue inclusive education has been resolved. The question of *how* has taken precedence. It can be answered by keeping abreast of new developments by accessing professional publications and web sites, attending conferences, visiting other schools and classrooms, or participating in workshops or trainings provided as professional development in your school.

Research suggests that teachers who have received training on research-based techniques are more likely to use them in their classroom when the following conditions are true

(Boardman, Arguelles, Vaughn, & Klingner, 2005; Gersten, Chard, & Baker, 2000; Gersten & Dimino, 2001; Vaughn, Klingner, & Hughes, 2000):

1. Teachers can see positive consequences for their learners.

2. The new techniques lead to improvements for the most challenging learners in the class.

3. The new techniques fit with the teacher's philosophy and general approach to teaching.

4. Implementation is feasible, even when common barriers (e.g., time) are present.

5. Preparation involves a high-quality sequence of theory–demonstration–practice, with ongoing support once use begins.

Ongoing support is a critical element of effective implementation. Coaching and mentoring by colleagues or consultants with advanced expertise have proven effective (Gersten & Dimino, 2001).

The purpose of this book is to draw attention to recommended and research-based practices that can be adopted and implemented by all schools. In reality, the translation of the professional literature into classroom practice is often an unmet expectation for a variety of reasons. The challenges of translating researched models, methods, or strategies into everyday practices have been described in the literature (Boardman et al., 2005; Gersten et al., 2000; Gersten & Dimino, 2001; Vaughn et al., 2000), with tension between researchers, administrators, and teachers too often the product. Teacher skepticism regarding the usefulness of published research is well known, and underlying reasons should be acknowledged. Published research may be perceived as highly technical and lacking clear implications for classroom practice. In other cases, teachers may not see an obvious connection between the setting and problem in a study and those in their own classrooms. To create a culture that values seeking, discussing, and implementing new practices, educational teams must see a direct relationship between new practices and improved student outcomes.

Provisions of the No Child Left Behind Act of 2001 (PL 107-110) that require schools to implement evidence-based practices have sparked considerable debate about what criteria should be applied to identify such practices. Box 2.1 describes the What Works Clearinghouse, which is operated by the U.S. Department of Education to identify programs and practices that meet rigorous criteria for evidence-based practice. Most of the research available to educational teams is found in textbooks, professional journals, conference presentations, and workshops. Practices that have been proven effective by one or more data-based studies are sometimes considered to be evidence based, but are more likely described as "promising" or "recommended"—terms used to describe practices that have been proven effective in data-based studies but which fall short of the more rigorous criteria applied by the National Center for Education Research, Institute of Education Sciences. In general, practitioners should prioritize new practices that have the most research support.

Probably the most pressing questions for practitioners are the following:

- What type of research is most helpful?
- Where can it be found?

The most helpful research would be that conducted in inclusive classrooms under typical conditions, with attention to effects on all learners. Studies that focus on learners with specific challenges, including English language learners and students with identified disabilities, are more abundant. Translating and importing techniques in these studies requires planning and collaboration between teachers and specialists. Because of the belief that only the general

Box 2.1. ⭐ What Works Clearinghouse

The *What Works Clearinghouse* (http://ies.ed.gov/ncee/wwc) is a web-based resource dedicated to the evaluation and dissemination of educational research, operated by the Institute of Education Sciences of the U.S. Department of Education. Established in 2002, the functions of the *What Works Clearinghouse* include establishing standards for evaluating research studies, evaluating existing research studies using rigorous criteria, and informing the public of the quality of research support interventions in specific areas of practice. Individual research studies are determined to meet evidence standards, meet standards with reservations, or not meet standards based on the extent to which the design of the research studies meet established criteria, which includes randomized assignment, limited attrition, and positive effect sizes. The evaluation criteria do not consider whether an intervention has been tested in an inclusive classroom.

To date, the *What Works Clearinghouse* has evaluated and summarized the existing research in the areas of beginning reading, early childhood education, dropout prevention, middle school math, elementary school math, interventions for English language learners, and character education.

or special educator or specialist can implement a technique, the learner often is pulled out of the classroom. Table 2.3 describes tips for facilitating translation of research to practice.

Seeking new ideas and strategies for inclusive classrooms is a vital aspect of leadership, especially given that inclusive education is a process that is undergoing constant evaluation and enhancement. Teams that seek and translate research–based methods on a routine basis are more likely to view inclusive education as a dynamic and flexible collection of practices that are constantly evolving in response to their learners' needs rather than interpret the ongoing search for new ideas as criticism of their current level of expertise.

ARRANGING FOR COLLABORATION

Collaboration between general and special educators has long been recognized as a requirement for, and indicator of, inclusive education (Dettmer, Thurston, & Dyck, 2005; Friend & Cook, 2006; Idol, 2002), with coplanning and coteaching being the most widely recommended collaborative practices. Although the importance of collaboration is widely accepted, it does not happen naturally. Leaders must take explicit steps to arrange for collaboration. Leadership is required in three facets of arranging collaboration: establishing a culture that fosters teamwork and shared expertise, creating structures for face-to-face interactions, and ensuring productive use of available coplanning time (Dettmer, Thurston, & Dyck, 2005; Friend & Cook, 2006; Idol, 2002; Murawski & Dieker, 2004; Villa, Thousand, & Nevin, 2008).

A collaborative culture is built on a belief in shared responsibility among team members for educating all learners. Collaboration works best when it is voluntary and when all involved share a mutual goal and respect for each other's expertise (Friend & Cook, 2006). These fundamental bases do not emerge organically whenever teams are formed; leadership is necessary to ensure their presence. Effective leadership sets expectations and provides

Table 2.3. General strategies for facilitating translation of research into practice

Nobody's perfect

- Emphasize whenever possible that effective inclusive schools are those that seek to understand and address their challenges and limitations, rather than waste time assigning blame or delaying action because no clear solution is available.

Skepticism is to be expected

- Acknowledge that many teachers do not perceive published research studies as relevant or helpful and ask team members to describe in what form (e.g., periodical, online, presenter) they prefer to access research.
- Acknowledge that practices that are evidence based do not work exactly the same for all learners; therefore the evidence that is most important is that which we gather in our own classrooms.

Custom fit

- Establish your school as a data-based environment in which decisions are made based on student outcome as determined by a variety of measures, not by subjective judgments or perceptions.
- Emphasize that translating research into practice is an important way to address challenges or problems identified by the team; it should therefore hold potential for an immediate impact on student achievement or behavior.
- Arrange for professional development that addresses needs identified by the team; make the staff active, rather than passive, participants in activities.

The force will be with you

- When new practices are introduced through professional development, teams should develop a plan for how they will integrate the new practice in the classroom.
- Establish what types of data will be used to determine impact of the new practice and ultimately whether the data addresses the challenges or problems that led to professional development.
- Emphasize that teachers will not be expected to continue practices that do not improve student outcomes as long as there is data to show lack of impact.
- Clarify whether teachers are expected to implement a new practice just as it was described in the research or professional development activity (with fidelity) or whether they can pick and choose elements or parts based on their perceptions of what will work best in their classrooms.
- Provide ongoing support following initial implementation by arranging for coaching or mentoring by experienced peers or by arranging for such supports from an outside resource, such as consultant or university faculty.

Make it a habit

- Include sharing of new ideas and practices on the agenda for regular team meetings.
- Include updates on implementation and impact of new practices on the agenda for regular team meetings.

structures, beginning with linking collaboration to the school's overarching mission and vision. Leadership activities that create structures for collaboration include forming teams and coteaching pairs before creating the schedule of courses and staffing, rather than developing a master schedule first and then expecting teams to find time to collaborate within that structure. Other leadership activities that can foster trust, respect, and goal sharing by team members include expanding traditional grade-level teams to include a special educator and specialists, as well as emphasizing the sharing of information and team participation in professional development. When team members resist collaboration, it is often because they view general educators and special educators as having specialized expertise of benefit only to "their kids." Leaders must emphasize that the expertise of both will be necessary to support an inclusive classroom; moving forward, the emphasis should be on evolving as members of a collaborative team, not as specialists.

Collaboration requires structures that facilitate face-to-face time between team members inside and outside of the classroom. The amount of time that team members have for coplanning outside of the classroom will determine what type of teaching arrangement is possible. Types of arrangements include the following (Friend & Cook, 2006):

- Coteaching, in which two teachers codeliver instruction
- Alternative teaching, in which each teacher delivers instruction to a smaller group of learners
- Station teaching, in which each teacher delivers one part of a lesson and students rotate between teachers
- Parallel teaching, in which the class is divided and each teacher instructs one half of the class
- One teaching and one observing/drifting, in which one teacher focuses on assisting learners who appear to be struggling

The last option often involves a special educator taking a passive helper role as the general educator delivers instruction. It is frequently a default arrangement when teachers are not able to plan outside of class.

For coteaching or team teaching to be successful, planning must occur outside of class. Coplanned lessons are more effective because they anticipate challenging content and build in instructional strategies and supports ahead of time, rather than waiting to see where learners struggle and provide help at that time. High school teams are often structured by content area (e.g., math, science), in which case assigning a special educator to a team allows that individual to gain more content-area expertise (Dieker, 2007). The potential benefit of this arrangement is demonstrated by the example of a special educator assigned to a math department who, with input from her colleagues, created a resource binder that included information needed to help students with common problems. She was able to use the resource to recognize when learners were making common mistakes and was confident in providing assistance within the flow of the class.

Structures that promote effective collaboration include the following:

- Including special educators on grade-level or "house" teams, with the expectation for full participation in all team activities (Kennedy & Fisher, 2001)
- Creating schedules that provide common planning times for team members (Murawski & Dieker, 2004)
- Establishing an expectation that general and special educators will codeliver instruction (Villa et al., 2008)
- Constructing IEPs for included learners with special needs with the intention of implementation and progress monitoring in the general education classroom (Dieker, 2007)

Creating collaborative structures can be challenging. One approach that can have negative consequences is clustering a larger number of learners with special needs in one classroom. The rationale for this arrangement is that it takes advantage of general education teachers who are motivated to serve learners with special needs and uses the special educator's time efficiently. Unfortunately, clustering undermines the goal of achieving natural proportions, meaning that the proportions of learners with special needs in a particular class should not exceed proportions in the entire school. The more subtle problem with clustering is that it isolates inclusive education to specific classrooms and hence undermines the goal of consistency discussed previously. Capper and Frattura advocated for "heterogeneous, proportional representation" in which the proportions of learners with special needs within each classroom match proportions for the entire school (2009, p. 24). Toward that goal, they recommended assigning students with disabilities first, separating students whose challenging behaviors might provoke other students, pairing English language learners with another

Table 2.4.   How to use coplanning time effectively

Implement general strategies

- Develop a routine for each session and don't get distracted by other issues.
- Generate a product for each session that each team member can refer to between meetings.
- Designate some time for looking ahead to upcoming units to allow time to seek out supplemental materials and resources.

Reference overarching goals

- Use materials and instructional methods that give each learner the best opportunity to meet your goals for the lesson.
- Design instruction to maximize in-class participation and learning and minimize the need for reteaching after class—or worse, assigning uncompleted work as homework.
- Anticipate concepts or skills that will be especially challenging for some learners, rather than waiting for failure.

Maximize team functioning

- Determine the coteaching arrangements that will maximize active participation of all team members.
- Determine what type of advanced preparation team members might need to fulfill their role in the lesson.
- Determine how each team member will implement the classroom management system and any behavior intervention plans for individual learners.

Address specific needs of learners

- Determine when specific individualized education program goals can be addressed and evaluated within the flow of the classroom routine.
- Determine when individualized instruction will be implemented and who will work directly with the learner.

speaker of the same language, and assigning language learners at different levels of acquisition in each classroom.

Leadership is required to ensure that collaborative planning time is used in a way that leads to observable changes in classroom instruction. Teams that are motivated to collaborate will benefit from using processes or tools that guide their thinking and decision making. Perceptions that the time allocated to coplanning is not productive can "turn off" dedicated team members or lead to the formation of separate teams-within-teams, which undermines the concept of shared accountability. Table 2.4 presents tips for making coplanning time as productive as possible. Teams may construct their own routine and meeting format or opt for published guides, such as *The Co-Teaching Lesson Plan Book* (Dieker, 2006). Table 2.5 presents general strategies for arranging collaboration in your school.

Although regular time together is required for teams to engage in coplanning, team members can make good use of intermittent blocks of time for longer-range planning, sharing of resources, professional development, or problem solving. Thousand and Villa (2005) proposed strategies for expanding time for collaborative planning, teaching, and reflecting (see Table 2.6).

REFLECTING ON PROCESSES AND OUTCOMES

Reflection has long been recognized as a trait of successful teachers and a strategy for continuous improvement. Self-questioning is a critical reflective behavior that is especially relevant for inclusive education teams who are seeking to meet a diverse set of needs and organize themselves into an effective "unit." Reflective practitioners use questioning to evaluate outcomes for students and to determine the extent to which they, their colleagues, the school, and the larger community achieved their purposes (York-Barr, Summers, Ghere, & Montie, 2005). Effective inclusive education requires continuous enhancement at the pro-

Table 2.5. General strategies for arranging for collaboration

Establish a collaborative culture

- Send a clear message that an inclusive education program designed and delivered through collaboration among school personnel, parents, and students is superior to one conceived by just a few.
- Administrators and specialists model collaboration with staff and take turns coteaching in classrooms.
- Incorporate collaborative behavior into the job descriptions and evaluation process for all staff.
- Send a clear message that although collaboration must be voluntary, it is expected that staff will put forth effort to resolve any issues that would prevent them from collaborating.
- Provide an atmosphere in which team members feel comfortable discussing issues and concerns regarding collaboration in their schools.
- Acknowledge positive examples of collaboration in your school.

Create collaborative structures

- Build class and staffing schedules by first designating time for all team members to meet together for problem solving and coplanning.
- Construct teams that include special educators and (when available) specialists.
- Create schedules for special educators that allow them to coteach in the general education classroom.
- Distribute learners with special needs across all classrooms in natural proportions.
- Create time for collaboration when sufficient time cannot be found.

Make good use of coplanning time

- Establish an agenda, routine, or template for teams to follow each time they meet.
- Establish a rule that time will be used for coplanning and the meeting should not be "hijacked" by other issues.
- Ensure that everyone who attends plays a part in planning and delivering the resulting lesson(s).

gram, classroom, and individual team member levels. Decisions about where enhancements are needed and how resources are allocated should be based on systematic reflection and formal evaluation of processes within the inclusive education program and outcomes for included learners. Processes include the ways in which decisions are made regarding school policies and practices, structures put into place to facilitate collaboration, and IEPs for learners with disabilities. The most important outcomes are those for the learner. Evaluation should consider both academic and social outcomes as measured through both qualitative and quantitative measures (see Table 2.7).

Reflection can involve a formal structure (e.g., journaling, discussing with peers, reviewing videos) or an informal strategy (e.g., taking time for self-questioning after a lesson or at the end of the day). Teachers use reflection to identify areas of success, as well as areas in which improvement is needed. For those in inclusive classrooms, the scope of self-questioning must be broad enough to encompass both the way in which the team delivered instruction and support, as well as the outcomes for the learners. The following are suggested questions:

- Were all learners able to gain access to and understand the content the way it was presented today?
- Were all learners able to meet expectations for whole-class, small-group, and/or individual seatwork today?
- How well did each learner perform on the assignments today?
- Do any learners seem to need more support to keep up with the rest of the class?
- Were all resources, including team members, used to their fullest potential today?

Evaluation involves a more systematic, comprehensive approach to collecting data on elements of an inclusive program and determining its overall level of success. The advantage

Table 2.6. Strategies for expanding time for collaborative planning, teaching, and reflection

Borrowed time
- Rearrange the school day to get a 50- to 60-minute block of time before or after school for coteachers to plan.
- Lengthen the school day for students by 15–30 minutes on 4 days, allowing for early student dismissal on the fifth day to gain a significant block of time (1–2 hours) for coteachers to meet.

Common time
- Ask coteachers to identify when during the day and week they prefer to plan, then redesign the master schedule to accommodate their preference with a block for common preparation.

Tiered time
- Layer preparation time with existing functions such as lunch and recess.

Rescheduled time
- Use staff development days for coteachers to do more long-range planning.
- Use faculty meeting time to problem solve common coteaching issues of immediate or long-range importance.
- Build at least one coteacher planning day into the school schedule each marking period or month.
- Build in time for more intensive coteacher planning sessions by lengthening the school year for teachers (not students) or by shortening the school year for students (not teachers).

Released time
- Go to year-round schooling with 3-week breaks every quarter; devote 4–5 days of each 3-week intersession to coteacher planning as professional development days.

Freed-up time
- Institute a community service component to the curriculum; when students are in the community (e.g., Thursday afternoons), coteachers meet to plan.
- Schedule "specials" (art, music, physical education), clubs, and tutorials during the same blocks (e.g., first and second periods) so that coteachers have at least that much extra time to plan.
- Engage parents and community members in conducting half-day or full-day exploratory, craft, hobby (e.g., gourmet cooking, puppetry, photography), theater, or other experiential programs to free time for coteachers to plan.
- Partner with colleges and universities; have their faculty teach in the school, provide demonstrations, or conduct university-campus experiences to free time for coteachers to plan.

Purchased time
- Hire permanent substitutes to free coteachers for planning during the day rather than before or after school.
- Compensate coteachers for spending vacation or holiday time on planning with either pay or compensation time during noninstructional school-year days.

Found time
- Strategically use serendipitous times that occasionally occur (e.g., snow days, student assemblies) to plan.

New time
- Determine ways that the school administration may provide coteachers with incentives that would motivate them to use their own time to plan.

From *Creating an Inclusive School* (2nd. ed., Figure 4.1, pp. 66–67), by Richard A. Villa & Jaqueline S. Thousand, Alexandria, VA: ASCD. © 2005 by ASCD; reprinted by permission. Learn more about ASCD at www.ascd.org

of a comprehensive evaluation is that it provides a "big picture" view of the collection of practices that inclusive education comprises. Schools may choose to develop their own evaluation tools and procedures, for which background knowledge of recommended practices is essential. Two evaluation instruments for inclusive education programs have been described in the professional literature. The Program Quality Measurement Tool (PQMT; Cushing et al., 2009) was designed to evaluate the quality of inclusive programs for learners with significant disabilities. The 44 indicators of the PQMT reflect recommended practices, with the degree of presence for an indicator rated on a 5-point scale. Sources of evidence include

Table 2.7. General strategies for reflecting on processes and outcomes

Start with a vision

- Always begin a class or lesson with a vision of how you want it to unfold and what the experience will be like for the learners in the class.
- Clarify specific goals you hope to achieve and determine what types of student behavior or work you will use to determine if your goals were met.

Stop and think

- Establish a routine for reflecting before planning the next day's lesson.
- Build reflection into the agenda or format for group meetings.
- Generate specific reflection questions that focus on outcomes for learners with special needs.
- Consider recording your reflections in a journal for later use.

When to be formal

- Establish a schedule for a more formal evaluation of your program.
- Select or create tools for gathering information that can be used to target areas of success and those in need of improvement.

See the big picture

- Remember that the goal of inclusive education is to provide the best "school experience" for learners, which means considering different types of data, including the learner's perspective on high notes and major disappointments.

Table 2.8. Indicators of the Program Quality Measurement Tool

Abbreviated indicator	Data sources			
	Administrator interview	Educator interview	Direct observation	Archival records
Local education agency level				
Key person identified to support staff working with students with severe disabilities	X	X		
Written plan for ongoing professional development				X
District mission reflects accountability for all students				X
School building level				
School's mission reflects accountability for all students	X			X
School's mission reflects community responsiveness	X			X
Students attend their neighborhood schools.				X
Students attend school in natural proportions.				X
All students are provided equal opportunities for recognition and access to school events.	X	X	X	
Classroom is located among other classrooms			X	
Staff communicate respectfully about students.	X	X	X	
Examples of high student expectations are observed throughout the school.			X	
Administrators and staff engage in active supervision during nonacademic times.	X	X	X	
A school improvement plan is developed, monitored, evaluated, and disseminated.				X

Abbreviated indicator	Data sources			
	Administrator interview	Educator interview	Direct observation	Archival records
Evidence of progress on the school improvement plan	X			X
All staff given professional development opportunities	X			X
Principal assumes responsibility for the school staff	X	X		
Administrators' values align with school mission.	X			
Educators are provided time to work together.	X	X		
Principal advocates for personnel/material resources	X	X		
All students participate in district and state assessments.				X
Special educators are members of each school team.	X	X		
Student level				
Formal and informal assessments are used to identify strengths, needs, and interests.	X			X
Student interests and preferences provide the basis for instructional content.		X		X
Transdisciplinary approach used to develop individualized education programs (IEPs) and conduct evaluations		X		X
Student's programs use integrated therapy models.		X	X	
Evidence of school–family communication exists.	X	X	X	
Student's program develops links with community agencies		X		X
Medical records are updated and adhered to by the staff.		X	X	X
Data are collected regularly, summarized, and reviewed by the IEP team to make program changes.		X		X
Functional behavioral assessments and behavior plans are implemented as needed.				X
Transition plans are written for students age 14 years and older.				X
Instructional content is relevant to student's daily life.			X	X
Students have opportunities to interact with peers.		X	X	X
Students are given opportunities to make choices.		X	X	X
Instructional materials vary across activities/days.		X	X	X
Instructional content is age appropriate.		X	X	X
Attention provided for engaging in appropriate behavior			X	
Students understand their educational routines.			X	
Various group learning strategies are used in learning.		X	X	
Strategies accommodate for students' learning styles.		X	X	
Students receive accommodations and adaptations.			X	X
Students enrolled in age-appropriate classrooms			X	
Multiple settings/people/materials are used for generalization of instruction.			X	X
Teachers and peers actively model how students should act in order to become more effective learners.		X	X	X

Republished with permission of Sage Publishing from "Evaluating Inclusive Educational Practices for Students with Severe Disabilities Using the Program Quality Measurement Tool" by Cushing et al., 2009, *Journal of Special Education, 42*, p. 198; permission conveyed through Copyright Clearance Center, Inc.

Table 2.9. Rating scale of components of a responsible inclusion program for students with high-incidence disabilities component and item

I. *Each student's educational needs are considered first*

1. Each student's academic progress and likelihood for success in an inclusion program influences placement in an inclusion program.
2. Each student's social progress and emotional needs influence placement in an inclusion program.
3. Alternative intervention models within the school are available for students who are not successful within an inclusion model.
4. Procedures for individually determining each student's progress in an inclusion setting are established and implemented.
5. Programs are designed to fit the needs of students rather than students forced to fit the established program.

II. *Teachers' skills, knowledge and attitudes toward inclusion classrooms*

6. General education teachers who teach in inclusion classrooms demonstrate beliefs and skills that facilitate their effectiveness in addressing the diverse needs of students with disabilities.
7. Teachers self-select their involvement in inclusion classrooms.
8. Teachers involved in coteaching participate in selecting their coteaching partner.
9. All teachers at the school identify the importance of accepting and valuing students.
10. Teachers (general and special education) exhibit an orientation to instruction for students with disabilities that indicates their responsibility for the student's success.

III. *Adequate resources are provided*

11. Inclusion programs are viewed as investments and not as ways to reduce special education costs.
12. Staff and administration are committed to providing the resources necessary to develop or maintain high-quality inclusion programs.
13. Adequate personnel are available to provide effective inclusion models.
14. Teacher-to-student ratio is adequate to meet the instructional and social needs of students with disabilities in inclusion classrooms.
15. Adequate materials and curricula are available to meet the needs of students with disabilities in inclusion classrooms.
16. Adequate technology is available to enhance learning of students with disabilities.

IV. *Inclusion models are developed and implemented at the school-base level*

17. School personnel are involved in the development and implementation of the inclusion model.
18. Teachers and key stakeholders perceive that the school level administrator is supportive of responsible inclusion programs.
19. The inclusion model reflects the needs of students in that school.
20. The implications of inclusion are considered for all school personnel.

V. *Parents are involved in the development and implementation of the inclusion model*

21. Parents' views are considered when students' service-delivery models are implemented.
22. A plan is in place to gain the support of parents in the community.
23. A systematic, ongoing method of communication is planned to ensure that parents are informed about the placement of their children.

VI. *A continuum of services is maintained*

24. School personnel realize that the needs of all students with high-incidence disabilities are unlikely to be met within the inclusion model.
25. Alternative services (e.g., resource, pull-out, self-contained classes) are available to meet the needs of students who are not progressing adequately within the inclusion model.
26. Students with disabilities are not placed in general education classrooms merely because alternative services are not available.

VII. The service delivery model is continually evaluated and altered

27. Procedures for evaluating the inclusion service delivery model have been identified and are systematically implemented.

28. Effective inclusion models for high-incidence disabilities that are implemented at other sites are visited so as to identify successful program components.

29. Procedures for fine-tuning and improving the inclusion model are considered on an ongoing basis.

VIII. Ongoing professional development

30. The skills and knowledge needed by all the professionals at the school are assessed and considered when designing professional development experience.

31. Professional development opportunities designed to meet the needs of all professionals, including support staff (e.g., cafeteria workers, after-school workers) are provided on an ongoing basis to enhance their skills with students with disabilities.

32. Opportunities to visit classrooms of teachers who are effectively meeting the needs of students with disabilities in inclusion settings are provided.

IX. Philosophy of inclusion is developed at the school level

33. Opportunities to discuss issues related to inclusion are provided for all key stakeholders in the school including teachers, parents, and support staff.

34. A written philosophy on inclusion exists that is endorsed by key stakeholders in the school.

35. The written philosophy on inclusion provides guidelines for the development of policy and service delivery models.

X. Curriculum approaches that meet the needs of all students are developed and refined

36. Appropriate instructional practices that increase active and intensive participation of students with disabilities in the learning tasks are implemented.

37. Teachers make instructional adaptations to meet the learning needs of students with disabilities.

38. Teachers make adaptations in materials to meet the learning needs of students with disabilities.

39. Adequate teacher time is allocated to meeting the needs of students with disabilities in the general education classroom.

40. Opportunities for reteaching or providing additional support for students with disabilities are evident.

XI. Roles and responsibilities of the special education teacher and other specialists

41. The roles and responsibilities of the special education teacher and other specialists (e.g., speech therapist) within the inclusion model are specified.

42. Adequate opportunity for the special education teacher and other specialists to provide direct and intensive education for students with disabilities is available.

43. Adequate time is available to coplan and collaborate with other professionals, including the general education teacher.

XII. Roles and responsibilities of the general education teacher

44. The role and responsibilities of the general education teacher within the inclusion model are specified.

45. Adequate opportunities for the general education teacher to provide appropriate instruction for students without disabilities are available.

46. Adequate time to coplan and collaborate with other professionals, including the special education teacher, is provided.

47. Special area teachers (art, music, physical education) are provided with training and support as related to the students with disabilities in their classes.

From "Using a Rating Scale to Design and Evaluate Inclusion Programs" by S. Vaughn, J.S. Schumm, & J.B. Brick, 1998, *Teaching Exceptional Children, 30,* p. 41. Reprinted with permission, copyright © 1998 by the Council for Exceptional Children, Inc. www.cec.sped.org. All rights reserved.

STAR ORGANIZER
STAR LEADERSHIP STRATEGY
GUIDING QUESTIONS

Table 2.10.

ACTION AREA	GUIDING QUESTIONS
 **Setting the tone**	• How does our school vision acknowledge a commitment to inclusiveness and to the success of all learners? • How well is our mission and vision understood by the entire school community? • How do members of the school community demonstrate equality and respect in the way they talk to and about learners with diverse abilities and needs? • How do school personnel demonstrate their shared responsibility for the success of all learners? • How and when does the decision-making process for the school take into account the impact for learners with diverse needs? • How do we ensure that students with diverse needs feel they are valued as members of the school community?
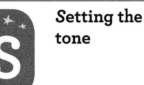 **Translating research into practice**	• How do we use data to determine which of our current practices are successful and should be used more consistently across inclusive classrooms? • How do we learn about new practices that could be helpful in our school? • How do we learn what types of professional development the educational teams need? • How do we support teams in implementing a new practice? • How do we ensure that new practices found to be effective are shared with the entire school and sustained over time?

interviews with administrators and teachers, direct observation, and review of records. The indicators and data sources for the PQMT appear in Table 2.8.

Based on their research with schools making the transition to inclusive programs, Vaughn, Schumm, and Brick (1998) created a rating scale of components of a responsible inclusion program for students with high-incidence disabilities (see Table 2.9). The instrument can be used in the design or evaluation of programs; the content was based on the authors' research with school sites. Several items indicate that some schools make abrupt transitions to inclusive programs without adequate planning and preparation. Vaughn et al. suggest the following 3-point scale for scoring each item: 3, *implements*; 2, *implements partially*; 1, *does not implement* or *implements poorly* (p. 42). As is the case with the PQMT, this evaluation instrument has not been normed and provides no suggested benchmarks. Thus, users must interpret their scores and decide on goals for improvement. Our suggestion is that schools

ACTION AREA	GUIDING QUESTIONS
 **Arranging for collaboration**	• How would we know if a learner was not experiencing academic or social success in our school? • How important does the staff perceive collaboration to be at our school? • How do we take full advantage of the expertise of the teachers and specialists? • What opportunities exist for team members to collaborate about how to instruct and support learners with special needs? • When do the general and special educators plan together for instruction in an inclusive classroom? • When do general and special education teachers coteach in a general education classroom? • How does our school engage parents as partners in maintaining an inclusive delivery model?
 **Reflecting on processes and outcomes**	• How do teams determine whether all learners are making progress in an inclusive classroom? • How do teams adjust when learners are not making progress? • What types of data do we use to ensure we are providing maximum access and maximum participation? • How and when do we solicit input from students and parents about the quality of our program? • How and when do we evaluate our program for presence of recommended practices?

adopt both short-term (e.g., 1-year) and longer term (e.g., 3-year) goals for improving their scores.

Chapter 6 includes an instrument to evaluate components of your own programs (see Tool 6.9). This template allows users to plug in specific program goals or components of significance in their school improvement plans, strategic plans, or plans associated with the inclusive vision for the school.

IMPLEMENTING THE STAR LEADERSHIP STRATEGY

The STAR leadership strategy is designed to stimulate leadership activity in four areas critical to inclusive education. Table 2.10 presents guiding questions for each of the four areas of practice. The following are suggestions for using the STAR leadership strategy.

At the District Level

- As a component of strategic planning
- As a guide for developing a mission and vision for the district
- As a tool for evaluating the inclusive education program
- As a tool to prioritize staffing needs and desired qualifications for new hires
- To help the school board understand the critical elements of effective inclusive education
- As a districtwide tool for guiding development of school improvement plans (SIPs)

At the School Building Level

- As a tool for designing and evaluating the inclusive education program
- As a guide for developing student and staff schedules
- As a component of the overall SIP
- To identify professional development needs
- To inform the position descriptions for administrators, teachers, and specialists
- To encourage leadership by administrators, teachers, and specialists

At the Individual Team Level

- As a guide for evaluating current services and identifying strengths and areas of need
- As a guide for developing schedules for team members and students
- To stimulate systematic reflection and evaluation of practices and clarification of professional development needs
- To encourage leadership by team members

Chapter 6 includes several tools for implementing the STAR leadership strategy. Tool 6.5 is a self-assessment for responding to each of the guiding questions (see Table 2.10). After completing this assessment, you will be prepared to complete the blank STAR Organizer (see Tool 6.3). Tool 6.4 is a modified organizer that includes the responsible leader and target dates. These tools are intended to expedite use of the STAR leadership strategy.

WRAPPING UP AND LOOKING AHEAD

In this chapter, we created the case for strategic leadership if inclusive education is to continue to evolve in our schools. The pursuit of inclusive education is supported by both philosophy and research, yet many schools are still seeking the expertise and leadership to make it a reality for learners. Chapter 3 focuses on leadership by principals and other administrators, as well as the "value-added" participation of peers and parents in your inclusive education program.

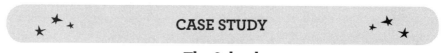

CASE STUDY

The School

Brewer Middle School serves approximately 450 students in Grades 6–8 in a smaller U.S. city. From its opening in 1959 through the 1980s, the school was considered to be one of the best schools in the city. Brewer was able to attract highly motivated teachers who appreciated both its ample resources and high-achieving student population. Learners with special needs were encouraged to attend a special school where they could receive the services they needed; thus, general education teachers were seldom required to address serious learning or behavioral challenges. However, since the 1980s, Brewer's community has become economically and culturally diverse, and all of the schools in the district now provide all or most special education services on site. The student population now includes English language learners and those with special needs, and the school has responded to the needs of these learners by building up their special education program and creating special programs for language learners.

The Principal

Ms. Angstrom took over as principal at Brewer 7 years ago, with a goal of maintaining the school's reputation as one of the best in the city. Toward that goal, she has spearheaded the following initiatives to be completed over the next year:

- *Implement a new schoolwide character education program to respond to concerns about bullying and to foster personal responsibility among students*
- *Revamp the curriculum in reading and writing to improve overall literacy*
- *Undertake curriculum mapping to align the math, social studies, and science curricula with the state learning standards*
- *Upgrade the use of technology through new purchases and staff development*
- *Develop a plan for meeting the new state requirements for response to intervention*

The Problem

Brewer has recently been notified of the following:

1. *The school did not meet adequate yearly progress requirements because of the performances of two subgroups: students with disabilities and English language learners.*

2. *The school is not meeting requirements for providing the least restrictive environment because less than 35% of those eligible for special education services spend at least 60% of their time in the general education classroom. That is, more than 65% are spending a majority of their day outside the general education classroom.*

The Approach

The school board for the district has directed Ms. Angstrom to address the above issues quickly. They also reiterated that the district is financially strapped and will not be able to approve any new positions. In meeting with a team of school leaders, including the special education director, it became obvious that to meet goals for improving performance and increasing inclusion, the entire school would have to share responsibility and work together—not as separate programs. Ms. Angstrom and her colleagues agreed to implement the STAR leadership strategy so that efforts are coordinated, leadership is distributed, and ways to measure improvements are clarified ahead of time.

IMPLEMENTING THE STAR LEADERSHIP STRATEGY

As a first step, Ms. Angstrom held a half-day meeting with the entire school staff to explain the four action areas of STAR. Smaller teams discussed the strategy, asked questions, and determined when they could meet again to discuss how well they were performing in each area and in what areas improvements were needed. The teams were given 1 week in which to provide input into each of the areas, after which Ms. Angstrom met with a group comprised of representatives from each team to summarize input and prioritize activities for each of the four practice areas. They then drafted proposed action items to be pursued by the school community. Following is a concise summary of the items for Brewer Middle School.

Setting the Tone

- *Form a communitywide group to craft a mission statement for the school that emphasizes a commitment to the success of all learners*
- *Create a vision for the school that includes full access and participation by all learners in the general education classroom and larger culture*
- *Emphasize the shared responsibility of all staff to educate learners with special needs in general education classrooms*
- *Create a letter to parents that explains the school's commitment to inclusive education and what steps will be taken to maximize success for all learners*

Translating Research into Practice

- *Emphasize that to be effective the entire school must acknowledge shortcomings and accept the challenge of improving classroom instruction*
- *Solicit input from staff on what type of professional development would be most helpful for serving included learners*
- *Ensure that groups currently working on initiatives for literacy curriculum adoption, enhanced use of technology in the classroom, and implementation of a character education program consider how new practices can be used to meet the needs of a diverse range of learners*

Arranging for Collaboration

- *Create teams that include special educators and specialists, with the expectation that teams will meet regularly*

- *Increase the number of cotaught classes, beginning with language arts and mathematics*
- *Create classrooms with natural proportions of learners with special needs*
- *Determine professional development needs as teams move toward co-planning and coteaching*

Reflecting on Processes and Outcomes

- *Survey students and parents regarding perceptions of the inclusive education program*
- *Incorporate review of student performance on classroom work into regular team meetings*

RECOMMENDED RESOURCES

Researched and Recommended Practices

Council for Exceptional Children (http://www.cec.sped.org)

Education Development Center (http://www.edc.org)

Inclusive Schools Network (http://www.inclusiveschools.org)

IRIS Center for Training Enhancements (http://www.iris.peabody.vanderbilt.edu)

National Center for Education Research, Institute for Education Sciences (http://www. ies .ed.gov/ncer/RandD/)

National Institute for Urban School Improvement, Consortium on Inclusive School Practices (http://www.urbanschools.org/publication/consortium_inclusive.html)

Office of Special Education and Rehabilitative Services, Research to Practice Division (http://www.ed.gov/about/offices/list/osers/osep/rtp.html)

Special Connections Project, University of Kansas (http://www.specialconnections.ku.edu)

The Association for Persons with Severe Handicaps (http://www.tash.org)

U.S. Department of Education, Institute for Educational Sciences, Regional Education Laboratory Program (http://www.ies.ed.gov/ncee/edlabs)

REFERENCES

Boardman, A.G., Arguelles, M.E., Vaughn, M.T., & Klingner, J. (2005). Special education teachers' views of research-based practices. *Journal of Special Education, 39*(3), 168–180.

Capper, C.A., & Frattura, E.M. (2009). *Meeting the needs of students with all abilities: How leaders go beyond inclusion* (2nd ed.). Thousand Oaks, CA: Corwin.

Cushing, L.S., Carter, E.W., Clark, N., Wallis, T., & Kennedy, C.H. (2009). Evaluating inclusive educational practices for students with severe disabilities using the Program Quality Measurement Tool. *Journal of Special Education, 42*(1), 195–208.

Dettmer, P., Thurston, L.P., & Dyck, N.J. (2005). *Consultation, collaboration, and teamwork for students with special needs* (5th ed.). Boston: Pearson.

Dieker, L. (2006). *The co-teaching lesson plan book* (3rd ed.). Whitefish Bay, WI: Knowledge by Design.

Dieker, L. (2007). *Demystifying secondary inclusion: Powerful school-wide and classroom strategies.* Port Chester, NY: DUDE Publishing.

Friend, M., & Cook, L. (2006). *Interactions: Collaboration skills for school professionals.* Boston: Allyn & Bacon.

Gersten, R., Chard, D., & Baker, S. (2000). Factors enhancing sustained use of research-based instructional practices. *Journal of Learning Disabilities, 33*(5), 445–457.

Gersten, R., & Dimino, J. (2001). The realities of translating research to practice. *Learning Disabilities Research & Practice, 16*(2), 120–130.

Idol, L. (2002). *Creating collaborative and inclusive schools.* Austin, TX: PRO-ED.

Kennedy, C.H., & Fisher, D. (2001). *Inclusive middle schools.* Baltimore: Paul H. Brookes Publishing Co.

Murawski, W.W., & Dieker, L.A. (2004). Tips and strategies for co-teaching at the secondary level. *Teaching Exceptional Children, 39*(5), 52–58.

No Child Left Behind Act of 2001, PL 107-110, 115 Stat. 1425, 20 U.S.C. §§ 6301 *et seq.*

Thousand, J.S., & Villa, R.A. (2005). Organizational supports for change toward inclusive schooling. In R.A. Villa & J.S. Thousand (Eds.), *Creating an inclusive school* (2nd ed.). Alexandria, VA: Association for Supervision and Curriculum Development.

Vaughn, S., Klingner, J., & Hughes, M. (2000). Sustainability of research-based practices. *Exceptional Children, 66*(2), 163–171.

Vaughn, S., Schumm, J.S., & Brick, J.B. (1998). Using a rating scale to design and evaluate inclusion programs. *Teaching Exceptional Children, 30*(4), 41–45.

Villa, R.A., & Thousand, J.S. (2005). *Creating an inclusive classroom* (2nd ed.). Alexandria, VA: Association for Supervision and Curriculum Development.

Villa, R.A., Thousand, J.S., & Nevin, A.I. (2008). *A guide to co-teaching: Practical tips for facilitating student learning.* Thousand Oaks, CA: Corwin.

Welch, A.B. (2000). Responding to student concerns about fairness. *Teaching Exceptional Children, 33*(2), 36–40.

York-Barr, J., Summers, W.A., Ghere, G.S., & Montie, J. (2005). *Reflective practice to improve schools: An action guide for educators.* Thousand Oaks, CA: Corwin.

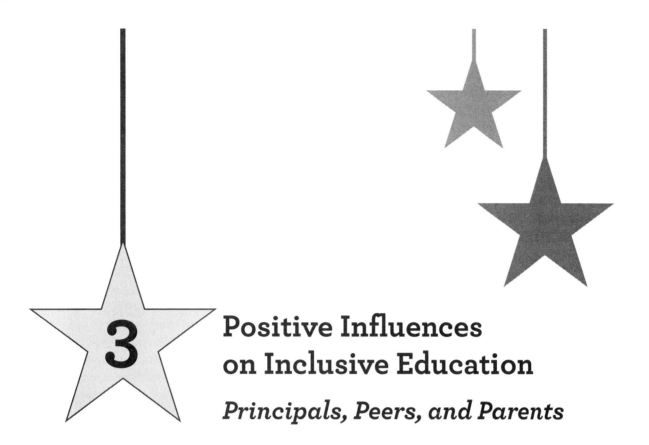

Positive Influences on Inclusive Education

Principals, Peers, and Parents

Research and discourse regarding inclusive education suggest that general and special educators are the key players in instructing and supporting learners with special needs. However, even the most dedicated and able teachers require supportive activity from the three groups that are recognized as potential positive influences on inclusive education: principals and other administrators, peers of learners with special needs, and the parents of learners with and without special needs. This chapter describes the contributions of these three groups to inclusive education, as well as leadership activities for maximizing their impact.

PRINCIPAL LEADERSHIP

Principal leadership has long been acknowledged as a necessary ingredient for school development and improvement. The principal's attitude toward inclusion has been identified as critical for successful implementation (e.g., Barnett & Monda-Amaya, 1998). More recent research on how principals' attitudes are shaped suggested that positive experiences with students with special needs and exposure to inclusive practices in training programs or via professional development are associated with more positive attitudes toward inclusion (Praisner, 2003). This study also found that less than 20% of principals surveyed had preparation for inclusive education and were significantly less likely to recommend inclusive placements for learners with emotional/behavioral disabilities or autism (Praisner, 2003). Thus, providing prospective principals (and other administrators) with knowledge of and experiences with positive examples of inclusion is critical to development of a positive attitude.

As the point person for the general education curriculum and culture, the principal exerts tremendous influence over the school's mission and use of inclusive practices. To be effective leaders, principals must possess knowledge and understanding of the legal foundations for special education practices and procedures. They must also recognize that special education is a set of services and support designed to meet a learner's needs, not a placement or a program. They should know how to include students with special needs into schoolwide assessments, as well as how to create a schoolwide culture that fully integrates special education learners and staff into the wider school community (McLaughlin & Nolet, 2004).

Principals are placed in the challenging situation of having to balance different initiatives and demands on a school's resources; they must make decisions regarding the best types of professional development and support to help staff implement new practices. For inclusive education to be effective, the principal must work in cohort with the special education administrators and teachers, not as counterparts in a separate program and culture. Fortunately, research on principal leadership suggests overlap between essential responsibilities for principals and the needs of inclusive education programs.

In a meta-analysis of research on leadership actions associated with improved student achievement, Marzano, Waters, and McNulty (2005) identified 21 responsibilities correlated with student academic achievement; those with the strongest relationship included situational awareness, flexibility, establishing procedures, outreach to stakeholders, and discipline. The researchers then considered which responsibilities were associated with implementing new practices (i.e., with change). They described two orders of change: first-order change, which is incremental and can be achieved within the existing structure and flow; and second-order change, which is more complex and involves changes in the way one conceptualizes issues or designs programs. The distinction between first- and second-order changes can also be observed in programs that have pursued limited-scope inclusive education or have physically included learners with special needs without committing to the underlying philosophy or sustained supports. Table 3.1 presents seven leadership responsibilities in order of their correlation with second-order change from the meta-analysis by Marzano et al. (2005), along with an example of how the responsibility is used in leadership for inclusive education. For most of the responsibilities, their relevance to leadership in inclusive education is obvious. The most important responsibility of possessing knowledge of the curriculum, instruction, and assessment may require a change in habits away from resources focused solely on traditional general education issues toward those addressing the needs of learners with diverse needs, including special needs. Indeed, the principal may serve as a model in reaching out for information from a variety of fields, including special education.

Are the expectations for the principal greater in an inclusive school? The reasoned answer is that the principal's job description is secondary to how responsibilities are met. Villa and Thousand (2005, p. 71) contrasted the traditional responsibilities of a principal with those in an inclusive school as follows:

1. Traditional model

    • Exercises responsibility for managing general education program
    • Places special education programs within general education facilities
    • Recognizes that program responsibility belongs to special education rather than general education

2. Inclusive model

    • Exercises responsibility for managing educational programs for all students
    • Articulates the vision and provides emotional support to staff members as they experience the change process
    • Participates as a member of collaborative problem-solving teams that invent solutions to barriers inhibiting the successful inclusion and education of any child
    • Secures supports to enable staff members to meet the needs of all children

Table 3.1. Principal leadership responsibilities for second-order change as applied to inclusive education

Leadership responsibility	Description of principal	Relevance to inclusive education
Knowledge of curriculum, instruction, and assessment	Is knowledgeable about curriculum, instruction, and assessment practices; is able to contribute to design and development of practices; and does not simply defer to others	• More effective leadership and support at IEP meetings. Principal participates in and guides IEP team discussions by providing clear information on the expectations for student learning and behavior at each grade level/subject area. (If we know the expectations for our students, we can better design instructional supports and adaptations.) • Understanding what teachers are expected to teach leads to better decisions about allocation of time and resources to support classroom teachers in providing successful inclusion experiences. • Prepares parents in advance of IEP meetings by helping them to understand specific curriculum or instructional requirements their children will face and necessary information for planning needed supports
Optimizer	Inspires and leads new and challenging innovations; consistently displays a positive attitude toward innovations; and supports staff efforts toward changing practices	• Facilitates the school's vision for inclusive practice • Through modeling, provides energy and motivation to sustain inclusive practice over the long haul • Guides and supports a problem-solving process that is guided by the needs of students but recognizes the pressures and demands felt by classroom teachers and parents • Models effective student advocacy for staff and parents
Intellectual stimulation	Ensures that staff is aware of recommended, effective practices; provides opportunities for staff to learn about and discuss concepts or practices described in the professional literature	• Shares research and "best practice" with staff and parents • Arranges for professional development activities at the team, department, or faculty meeting level • Works with staff and parents to identify the academic and behavioral needs of students and then aligns professional development opportunities with identified priorities
Change agent	Demonstrates willingness in challenging the "status quo" and questioning the effectiveness of traditional practices; models or supports risk taking with initiatives that may prove beneficial	• Encourages/gives permission for risk taking by teachers • Facilitates team discussions that match data-based needs with research-based initiatives • Distributes leadership and decision making to include key stakeholders in the school community • "Speaks truth to power": advocates for needed changes when interacting with central administration
Monitoring/ evaluating	Closely monitors the effectiveness of the school's practices—particularly their impact on student achievement	• Works with school staff to organize ongoing assessment of learning and behavior across grades and subjects • Aligns assessments of students who have IEPs with learning standards for all students as well as for individual progress on goals • Uses data to set goals and monitor progress • Integrates data analysis as a regular component of professional development
Flexibility	Able to adapt style and exert directiveness/nondirectiveness as called for by the situation; encourages expression of differing opinions and is not rigid when challenged	• Provides opportunities for staff to exert leadership • Solicits input from staff on an ongoing basis • Models decision making that is consistently focused on the needs of students first and foremost
Ideals/beliefs	Can articulate well-defined beliefs about teaching and learning; demonstrates behaviors that are consistent with beliefs; uses beliefs to guide decision making	• Guides staff and parents to revisit core beliefs about inclusive education on a regular basis • Works with staff to ensure that inclusive values are visible to all students and school visitors

Source: Marzano, Waters, and McNulty (2005). *Key:* IEP, individualized education program.

Responsibility for the general education program expands to responsibility for the education of all students—a marked change from the traditional roles in which the special education administrator maintains primary responsibility for learners with special needs, even when they spend all or most of their days in the general education classroom. Effective principals accept responsibility for the achievement of all learners and recognize that they are better able to meet that objective by collaborating with the special education administrator and IEP team.

Research on turnover and retention indicates that teachers are more likely to leave their position when they believe that they are not supported by their principal (Billingsley, 2005; Guarino, Santibanez, & Daley, 2006). When a teacher or team decides that the general education classroom is not the least restrictive environment for an included learner, support from the principal is expected. In most cases, the team will have engaged in problem solving to preserve the placement and will have data indicating that the learner's academic or behavioral needs cannot be met in the general education classroom. But sometimes, evidence of attempts to address problems will be incomplete. In this case, the principal is put in the position of either supporting the recommendation as a means of supporting the staff or recommending that the team undertake problem solving, with a goal to facilitate success in the general education classroom. The latter scenario can be uncomfortable, particularly when it unfolds during a meeting with parents present. Principals can seek to avoid such a scenario by ensuring that teams are aware of the criteria and supporting evidence that should be used in making decisions regarding the appropriateness of the general education classroom. Then, discussion regarding evidence that a more restrictive setting is more appropriate will be interpreted as professional and consistent with the school's mission—not as a lack of confidence or support.

ROLES FOR ALL ADMINISTRATORS

The role of general education administrators—specifically superintendents, principals, and curriculum leaders—in inclusive education is critical, especially when a distributed model of leadership is desired. Top administrators are prepared to make important decisions and to drive the implementation of policies and initiatives. For many, leadership skills that are used effectively in their current positions are also useful for expanding efforts toward a more inclusive school.

Much has been written about the characteristics of school leadership, with notable researchers focusing on the requirements for higher student achievement (Marzano et al. 2005; Reeves, 2006), more inclusive programs (Capper & Frattura, 2009; Thousand & Villa, 2005), or differentiation of curriculum and instruction (Tomlinson & Allan, 2000). Regardless of whether the outcomes of concern are academic achievement or a broader measure of school quality (including inclusiveness), effective leaders are recognized for the abilities described in the following sections.

Walking the Talk

Leaders should recognize that they must be role models for the innovations they espouse for their stakeholders; their actions are more important than their words. Skeptics are watching for examples of inconsistency or evidence that the leader is not personally committed to what he or she is advocating. The importance of "walking the talk" may be especially true in the case of inclusive education, for which administrators may emphasize the importance of supporting learners with special needs in the general education setting, but then fail to provide the necessary resources for educational teams or revert back to using separate classrooms or services in response to the pressure of NCLB targets or challenging behavior. *Walking the talk* means living out the school's mission and vision, highlighting positive examples in the school community, and quickly addressing barriers that prevent maximum participation by learners with special needs. For some administrators, walking the talk may require sustained focus even when they are being evaluated primarily on different outcomes, namely test scores. New staff members are chosen based on their commitment to and expertise with inclusive education, and all employees are held accountable for implementing the school's mission and vision.

Guiding Questions for Administrators

- Do I believe in inclusiveness as a core value for my school?
- How do the stakeholders in my school know I am committed to our mission and vision for inclusive education?
- When have I modeled for stakeholders the attitudes and behaviors I expect from them?
- What action have I taken to hold others accountable for our mission?

Knowing What Counts

Effective school leaders initiate change with a clear vision of what the results will look like for all involved stakeholders. For new practices to be sustained, the effects must be obvious to learners, team members, and parents. Thus, leaders should identify "what counts" from the beginning. They should use data to determine whether new practices are working or if it is time for a change. They should make clear how success will be determined; this is especially important for inclusive education because stakeholders may hold different views of what constitutes a positive school experience for an included learner. As discussed in Chapter 2, outcomes for inclusive education are broader than test scores; participation in the school community and satisfactory social relationships may be more difficult to measure. Examples of key indicators include time in the general education setting, progress on IEP goals, academic achievement, student and parent perceptions, collaborative working relationships, and progress on adequate yearly progress targets. Multiple measures are necessary to attain a holistic view of the learner's achievement. Progress over years can be tracked by comparing outcomes for cohort groups over multiple years.

Monitoring what counts requires a practical and manageable protocol that yields helpful information between more formal program evaluations (as discussed in Chapter 2). Regular monitoring of key indicators maintains focus on inclusive practice with minimal resources. Figure 3.1 presents a sample protocol for monitoring progress on key indicators of inclusive education. In this example, the goal for time spent in the general education classroom is 80%—a percentage that some readers will consider too low and others will consider unattainable. Schools must establish their own target based on current percentages and a vision for improvement over multiple years.

Effective leaders also recognize that veteran teachers and specialists have grown accustomed to new initiatives that do not involve a shared understanding of how success will be determined or that involve implementing a new practice as the end goal, with little attention to actual impact on learners and their teachers. Resistance to new ideas is often the result of

---

Percent of students in general classroom >80% of the day:
- Summarized by grade level
- Reported by IEP case managers or district data manager
- Collected once annually

Percent of students meeting IEP progress benchmarks:
- Summarized by grade level
- Reported by IEP case managers
- Collected each grading period

Academic engagement is occurring at expected level of teachers:
- Summarized by grade level
- Reported by classroom teachers in team meetings or by online survey
- Reported by parents by online survey
- Collected three times annually

Social engagement is occurring at expected level of teachers:
- Summarized by grade level
- Reported by classroom teachers in team meetings or by online survey
- Reported by parents by online survey
- Collected three times annually

Accommodations, modifications, and adult support are appropriate for the needs of students:
- Summarized by grade level
- Reported by teachers in team meetings or by online survey
- Reported by parents by online survey
- Collected three times annually

Figure 3.1.   Sample monitoring protocol with key indicators. (*Key:* IEP, individualized education program.)

too many poorly implemented initiatives—not a desire to keep doing things the same way because it is comfortable. Innovations that produce results that teachers can see and that allow teachers to gain confidence in their ability to serve learners with diverse abilities will be taken seriously by those who are in the best position to make a difference. Leaders who regularly refer to data in team meetings or as rationale for new initiatives are demonstrating a commitment to knowing what counts.

Guiding Questions for Administrators

- How does our school define success for our inclusive education program?
- What schoolwide assessments yield data we can use to evaluate the success of our program?
- How do we track the impact of new initiatives or practices?
- How do administrators model and support the use of different types of data to make decisions?

Pitch a Large Tent

Leaders model their commitment to inclusiveness when they invite input and participation from all corners of the school community—and especially from members with different perspectives. For establishing the mission and vision for the school, the "tent" should include community members, parents, and students (with and without special needs), as well as broad representation from the school personnel in different positions. In many cases, stakeholders who are not in the school on a regular basis are not aware of its successes and challenges; however, once informed, they can act as advocates or ambassadors in the wider community. A public commitment to inclusiveness can serve as a bridge to the community and result in increased pride and investment by parents and community members.

Pitching a large tent also applies when addressing school issues or pursuing a change in practice. Leaders seek and accept input from those with different expertise and positions within the school not only because they are seeking "buy-in" once a decision is made, but also because they believe that the combined thinking of many is superior to that of just one or two. Modeling tolerance and respect for differences sends a clear and positive expectation for inclusive education.

Guiding Questions for Administrators

- When does our school pitch a big tent for discussion of the mission and success of our school?
- How do stakeholder groups participate in the life of our school?
- When do I demonstrate a commitment to inclusiveness within my duties as an administrator?
- How can I expand our tent to improve the quality of our inclusive education program?

Playing the Lead and Supporting Roles

Effective administrators are able to move between being the point person out in front of the rest of the team and leading from the rear, in which others take the lead. Taking the lead is desirable when team members lack the expertise or confidence to implement an initiative and will benefit from having an administrator model what is expected. In contrast, leading from the rear involves empowering and supporting team members to serve as the point person for innovation, with the understanding that an administrator is monitoring their progress and available to provide support. Empowering team members is advantageous when they possess the expertise and motivation to pursue innovation and can function as a team to use their combined talents. Although it may seem that leading from the rear is timesaving for administrators, the reality is that monitoring and supporting motivated professionals can be more challenging than taking charge. The benefits are that team members will undertake innovation from the perspective of the implementer and with background knowledge about the school and students. In addition, teams who have been empowered to implement change are more likely to sustain new practices and serve as models for colleagues. For most, achieving the optimal balance between leading from ahead and from behind is an ongoing quest.

Although the decision of how to lead is made in response to the needs of stakeholders, administrators can anticipate opportunities for both approaches. It is critical that administrators be visible leaders and supporters for inclusive education in the school community. A commitment to inclusiveness must be made from the top to be taken seriously; administrators must be poised to serve as the public face for their inclusive education program. On the other hand, when innovation involves areas in which team members have expertise, such as curriculum or instructional methods, a lead-from-behind approach is advantageous.

Guiding Questions for Administrators

- What opportunities do staff in our school have to assert leadership and responsibility to carry out initiatives and set goals?
- How is teacher leadership supported by the administration?
- How do leaders recognize when they must serve as the point person for their staff?

Principals and other administrators play crucial roles in the quality and sustainability of inclusive education programs. The professional literature has described strategies that will work for those who are ready and willing to accept leadership roles that are visible and supportive for students, parents, and staff.

STAR ORGANIZER FOR PRINCIPAL LEADERSHIP

Table 3.2 provides sample leadership activities for maximizing the impact of the principal and other administrators on your inclusive education program. Readers may find these activities suitable for their own situation, but are encouraged to use the self-assessment tool in Chapter 6 (Tool 6.5) to identify activities targeting their unique needs.

PEER FRIENDSHIP AND SUPPORT

Satisfactory peer relationships are one measure of successful inclusion; they may be valued equally with academic achievement by parents. Unfortunately, learners with special needs are at greater risk for unsatisfactory peer interactions and friendships, as well as more serious problems of bullying. Educational teams can facilitate positive interactions by modeling respectful behavior toward all learners and implementing programs or interventions designed to facilitate positive interactions, including those that involve peers as models and teachers.

For learners with significant needs, peers may provide academic support and opportunities for social interaction. With appropriate training, peers of learners with significant needs have provided both academic and social supports in general education classrooms at the elementary, middle, and high school levels (Carter, Cushing, & Kennedy, 2008). With training, peers have been able to provide academic assistance, including adapting or modifying assignments; paraphrasing lectures; providing prompting and corrective feedback; modeling appropriate behavior during group work; and facilitating positive social behaviors, including initiating and extending conversations (Carter, Cushing, Clark, & Kennedy, 2005; Carter & Kennedy, 2006; Cushing & Kennedy, 1997; Kennedy & Itkonen, 1994; Shukla, Kennedy, & Cushing, 1999). As "natural" supports, peers may provide the types of assistance otherwise provided by the teacher or paraprofessional, and learners with special needs may be more motivated to work with a peer than with an adult. Peers who support classmates with special needs may also improve on their own classwork, creating a "win-win" outcome for all (Cushing & Kennedy, 1997). Appropriate selection and training of peers is vital for success, and research suggests that support from multiple peers adds to the benefit (Carter et al., 2005).

One strategy for promoting positive social interactions among learners with moderate to severe disabilities and their high school peers is to facilitate friendships. The Peer Buddy

STAR ORGANIZER

FOR MAXIMIZING PRINCIPAL LEADERSHIP

Table 3.2.

AREA OF PRACTICE	SAMPLE LEADERSHIP ACTIVITIES
Setting the tone	• Highlight inclusive values during back-to-school night, opening institute days, and faculty meetings (e.g., school mission, inclusion goals). • Organize a leadership team that includes staff, parents, and students in order to guide and integrate current school initiatives. • Write position descriptions for all staff that include expectations for supporting learners with special needs.
 *Translating research into practice*	• Follow the general guidelines in Chapter 2 (Table 2.3) for identifying, implementing, and evaluating new practices. • Organize meetings of principals from different schools to share resources, ideas, and experiences in providing leadership in inclusive efforts. • Collaborate with university faculty to pursue grants or partnerships that will provide professional development and resources for educational teams.
 **Arranging for collaboration**	• Create regular opportunities for principals to meet with educational teams to discuss issues related to inclusive education in their school. • Assign students with special needs to a general education classroom even if they receive instruction outside the classroom for a part of the day. • Principals take turns coteaching a lesson in different classrooms.
 **Reflecting on processes and outcomes**	• Analyze system-level data at regular intervals to define strengths and problem areas with inclusion efforts. • Facilitate team, department, or advisory group meeting for system-level problem solving.

program (Hughes et al., 1999) involves a structured curriculum that guides schools through the process of recruiting, developing, and evaluating peers who form friendships with learners with significant disabilities (Hughes & Carter, 2008). As natural supports, peer buddies spend time socializing with their buddy and serve as the conduit for interactions with other peers, as well as role models and teachers, for many survival skills. Buddies interact inside and outside of the classroom, engaging in age-appropriate activities in the school community. Participants receive a Peer Buddy handbook that provides information and resources to increase knowledge and awareness of disability-related issues and ideas of activities (Hughes & Carter, 2008). Schools may recruit students by designating the program as a service learning opportunity for which credit is earned. Research indicated positive benefits for both students involved (Copeland et al., 2002, 2004; Hughes et al., 2001). Figure 3.2 summarizes the

---

For general education students:
- Develop new friendships
- Increase their advocacy skills and awareness of disability issues
- Gain additional knowledge about people in general and those with disabilities
- Learn enhanced interpersonal skills
- Experience personal growth and a sense of accomplishment
- Develop an interest in pursuing a career in human services
- Increase their expectations of peers with disabilities
- Learn from students with disabilities who are positive role models
- Have fun

For students with disabilities:
- Develop new friendships
- Gain opportunities for social interactions with peers
- Acquire important academic, social, and life skills
- Spend time with age-appropriate role models
- Receive effective peer support in general education settings
- Increase their independence and self-confidence
- Have fun

For teachers:
- Receive additional assistance from peer buddies in individualizing instruction for students with disabilities
- Experience professional growth and personal satisfaction
- Provide socializing opportunities for all students
- Experience increased diversity in the classroom

For administrators:
- Improve the school climate by supporting practices that foster a caring school community
- Align school practices with school reform efforts and legislation related to inclusion

For parents:
- Experience increased enthusiasm for their children's schooling
- Appreciate their children's growth and expanded social interactions and friendships

---

Figure 3.2.   Benefits associated with Peer Buddy programs. (From Hughes, C., & Carter, E.W. [2008]. *Peer buddy programs for successful secondary school inclusion* [p. 49]. Baltimore: Paul H. Brookes Publishing Co.; reprinted by permission.)

positive benefits of the Peer Buddy program for students, teachers, parents, and the school administration and community.

STAR ORGANIZER FOR MAXIMIZING PEER SUPPORTS

Potential leadership activities for maximizing the impact of peer supports for included students are described in Table 3.3. Because students play the critical roles, they should be involved in decisions regarding implementation.

STAR ORGANIZER

FOR MAXIMIZING PEER SUPPORTS

Table 3.3.

AREA OF PRACTICE	SAMPLE LEADERSHIP ACTIVITIES
 **Setting the tone**	• Highlight the importance of social interaction and peer relationships as a normal part of a positive school experience for all students, including those with special needs. • Articulate an expectation that cocurricular activities in the school will be accessible for all students.
 **Translating research into practice**	• Follow the general guidelines in Chapter 2 (Table 2.3) for identifying, implementing, and evaluating new practices. • Ensure that all staff are aware of the increased risk of social isolation for learners with special needs and the important roles they can play in facilitating positive peer relationships, including implementing evidence-based programs for peer supports.
 **Arranging for collaboration**	• Arrange for general and special educators to discuss issues related to the full participation in the culture of the school, including cocurricular activities. • Emphasize the shared responsibility of all staff to share information and work together to intervene on negative social interactions between students with special needs and their peers.
 **Reflecting on processes and outcomes**	• Form a committee that includes students and staff charged with monitoring the cocurricular opportunities and sense of belongingness for all students and making recommendations to the school leaders for new opportunities. • Solicit input from included learners on how welcomed they feel in the school and how satisfied they are with formal or informal peer supports.

PARENT INVOLVEMENT

Parent involvement has long been recognized as an important factor in the overall success of a school, and considerable attention has been paid to increasing involvement as a means to improve student outcomes. The link between parent involvement and student outcomes was acknowledged in the NCLB: Schools that receive Title I funds but do not demonstrate adequate yearly progress must enhance parent involvement by establishing a parent involvement policy developed collaboratively with parents, convening an annual meeting of parents, and developing school–parent agreements that outline actions to be taken by the school and parents to improve learner performance. Inclusive schools recognize that parent involvement is both a method and an outcome for building strong partnerships with the wider community, and that parents are perhaps the most important support for learners with special needs.

Benefits of Parent Involvement

Research has identified the following benefits of parent involvement (Epstein, 1995; Epstein et al., 2002; Henderson & Berla, 1994; Henderson & Mapp, 2002; Michigan Department of Education, 2001; Nathan, 1996; Speth, Saifer, & Forehand, 2008):

1. Benefits for students

   - Increased awareness of family supervision and respect for parents
   - Improved academic performance (e.g., homework, grades)
   - Improved attitude about school and self-esteem
   - Better understanding of how school works and how to self-advocate
   - Decreased likelihood to exhibit discipline problems or use drugs or alcohol
   - Improved skill in interacting with adults
   - Better understanding of parent representation in school decisions
   - Increased opportunities for enrichment and cocurricular activities

2. Benefits for parents

   - Improved understanding of how children learn and develop
   - Increased confidence in own ability to be an effective parent
   - Increased ability to assist their child with school work
   - Increased support from other parents
   - Better understanding of general school operations and how to access programs and services inside and outside the school
   - Understanding of parents' roles in carrying out the school's mission and vision
   - Feeling of shared ownership as member of school community
   - Ability to interact confidently with school personnel

3. Benefits for teachers and schools

   - Better understanding of students' backgrounds, culture, and family view of education
   - Understanding of specific strengths and challenges of families in the school community
   - Extra resources to assist in classroom or provide additional opportunities inside and outside of classroom

- Improved teacher morale
- Higher ratings of teachers by parents
- Higher student achievement
- Enhanced reputation in the community
- More opportunity to share mission and vision with community

Types of Involvement

In her extensive work on parents and schools, Epstein (1995) described six types of parent involvement that produce positive outcomes. Table 3.4 presents these six types of involvement and their relevance to inclusive education.

PARENTS' QUESTIONS ABOUT YOUR INCLUSIVE PROGRAM

Research suggests that parents of learners with and without special needs have questions and concerns regarding inclusive placements that must be addressed for effective school–parent relationships (Salend, 2006). Many concerns can be addressed by providing a clear description of your school's mission and vision, as well as information about features of the program designed to promote effective inclusion. Parents of peers may have concerns about how the presence of learners with special needs will affect the general functioning of the classroom or create competition for teacher attention (Giangreco, Edelman, Cloninger, & Dennis, 1993). Parents of learners with special needs may have more specific questions related to services for their child, such as how provisions of the IEP can be sustained in the general education classroom, how peers will interact with their child, and who will be the primary contact for the parents (Palmer, Fuller, Arora, & Nelson, 2001).

Informational meetings for parents and guardians are generally recommended for building a sense of community; they may be particularly important when implementing or enhancing your inclusive education program (Salend, 2006). Whether your school is making the transition to a more inclusive model or just reaffirming an existing mission, all school personnel should be able to respond to parents' questions and concerns in an accurate and respectful manner. Stivers, Francis-Cropper, and Straus (2008) described a calendar of activities designed to educate parents about your inclusive education program throughout the year. One activity includes establishing a resource center for books and materials that involve characters with special needs. Figure 3.3 provides a self-assessment for your ability to answer questions commonly asked by parents, including those of students with and without special needs.

In Chapter 6, we provide a mechanism for soliciting feedback from parents of students regarding your special education program—in particular the aspects of the program designed to facilitate successful inclusion (see Tool 6.7).

MAXIMIZING PARENTS' INVOLVEMENT

The first step to maximizing parents' involvement is establishing the following "preconditions" involving attitudes and expectations (Michigan State University, 2004). Principals, teachers, and staff should

- Understand the importance of the parents' role in the process of educating children
- View parents as experts on their children and as equals
- Understand that parents' attitudes toward school affect their children's attitudes

Table 3.4. Types of parent involvement and implications for inclusive education

Types of involvement and goals	Examples of school activities	Implications for inclusive education
Parenting *Goal:* Help all families establish home environments to support children's development.	• Provide information (via classes, workshops, videos, home visits) that describe child development and effective parenting practices. • Provide information on how parents can further their education or receive special training.	• Help parents prepare their child for the expectations of the general education setting and foster self-advocacy and self-determination skills. • Help parents develop skills and confidence for parenting their children with special needs.
Communicating *Goal:* Design effective forms of communication about school services and learner progress.	• Hold conferences with parents and provide translators and child care to encourage full attendance. • Distribute useful information on a regular schedule using print, phone, and live communications.	• Help parents understand the IEP process and how they can communicate effectively with the educational team. • Include parents in the ongoing monitoring of your inclusive practices. • When necessary, meet with parents in advance to prepare for complex educational decisions for their child.
Volunteering *Goal:* Recruit and organize parent help and support.	• Implement classroom volunteer programs with survey of parent interests and availability. • Recruit parent patrols to promote safety.	• Take steps to encourage parents of students with special needs or those with language or cultural differences. • Allow parents to talk with the class about their child's special needs.
Learning at home *Goal:* Provide information and ideas to families about how to help learners at home with homework, choices about classes and programs, and planning for the future.	• Provide information on curricular objectives, homework practices, and calendars at beginning of year. • Provide background information parents need to help with homework or provide follow-up instruction. • Involve parents in setting goals and planning for future.	• Help parents anticipate when their child will need help on specific types of assignments. • Allow parents to prepare their child for activities that will require challenging social-emotional skills.
Decision making *Goal:* Include parents in school decisions and developing parent leaders and representatives.	• Empower PTO/PTA groups to participate in decision making for school. • Form advisory groups to work on specific issues or provide ongoing monitoring of programs.	• Involve parents in the development of a mission and vision for inclusive education. • Include a parent advisory group in the monitoring of inclusive practices.
Collaborating with the community *Goal:* Identify and integrate community resources and services to strengthen school, families, and student learning and development.	• Provide information to families on community health, cultural, social support, academic support, or recreational programs or services. • Provide information on how learners and families might provide service in their school or community.	• Help parents link to support groups. • Point out resources for specialized therapies and services. • Inform parents of opportunities for service and learning opportunities that may foster social-emotional growth.

Source: Epstein (1995).
Key: IEP, individualized education program.

Self-Assessment

Use the following scale to score your level of preparedness to respond to commonly asked questions about inclusive education with clear, accurate, and confident responses. If you are in a leadership position, assess how well you have prepared others to respond.

Scores: 1 = Fully prepared
2 = Somewhat prepared but not very confident
3 = Have not thought about how I would respond

Common Questions from All Parents

1. How will my child be affected by a mission to provide inclusive education?
2. Why is the school adopting an inclusive education mission?
3. How will the school make sure that all students are getting what they need for high achievement?
4. Are there some students who are better served in another classroom?
5. How will we know if it works? What happens if it doesn't work?

Common Questions for Parents of Learners with Special Needs

1. How will my child's needs be met in the general education classroom?
2. How will my child's IEP be implemented in the general classroom?
3. My child is doing well in a special classroom; why increase time in the general classroom now?
4. My child is not doing well; how will increased time in general education address the challenges?
5. How will the general educator be prepared to work with my child?
6. What will happen if the other students make my child feel uncomfortable or unwelcomed?

Figure 3.3. Preparing to answer parent questions regarding inclusive programs. (*Key:* IEP, individualized education program.)

- Recognize the strengths of families raising children under adverse circumstances, including parents who are in poverty, incarcerated, divorced, or experiencing domestic violence
- Expect to have personal contact with parents

Inclusive schools recognize that the above preconditions must exist for all parents, including those from different cultures, backgrounds, and languages, as well as those who may not initiate contact with their children's schools. Numerous strategies for maximizing the six types of parent involvement can be found in the Recommended Resources section at the end of this chapter.

STAR ORGANIZER FOR MAXIMIZING PARENT INVOLVEMENT

Suggested leadership activities for maximizing the contributions of parents to your inclusive program are provided in Table 3.5. Readers are encouraged to consider the unique strengths and challenges of their own schools when identifying and prioritizing leadership activities in each of the four areas of STAR.

WRAPPING UP AND LOOKING AHEAD

In dedicating this chapter to principals, peers, and parents, we sought to highlight the significant impact of individuals who may be less recognized than teachers and specialists in the literature regarding inclusive education. Principals have an opportunity to not only fulfill

STAR ORGANIZER
FOR MAXIMIZING PARENT INVOLVEMENT

Table 3.5.

AREA OF PRACTICE	SAMPLE LEADERSHIP ACTIVITIES
 **Setting the tone**	• Highlight the importance of parent involvement in the school's mission and vision statements. • Establish a parent–teacher advisory group to guide efforts to improve inclusive practices.
Translating research into practice	• Follow the general guidelines in Chapter 2 (Table 2.3) for identifying, implementing, and evaluating new practices. • Generate a parent newsletter and web page that promotes positive parent involvement through use of evidence-based strategies.
 **Arranging for collaboration**	• Use structures (e.g., PTO) involving staff and parents to explore ways in which they collaborate to promote the inclusive mission of the school. • Involve parents in the major decision-making committees in the school.
 **Reflecting on processes and outcomes**	• Conduct an annual survey of parent satisfaction with their involvement in the school. • Clarify the types of "data" that can be used to evaluate both the amount and quality of parent involvement, with special attention to maximizing the positive impact—not just the number of hours.

their critical roles, but to ensure that peers and parents are also incorporated into the inclusive environment. Integrating peers as supports helps to disseminate the school's mission and vision while also providing cost-efficient, effective social support that helps to balance emphasis on academic achievement and facilitate a holistic view of inclusiveness. Informing and involving parents is a logical and effective means to communicate mission and vision throughout the larger community and to empower parents to become stakeholders in their school.

In Chapter 4, we move from general strategies that benefit all students to strategies tailored for students with unique needs. We sharpen our focus on learners who receive special education services and have an IEP. For these students, the IEP process provides opportunities to enhance their inclusion in the general education curriculum through active participation and constant attention to how the supports provided by the IEP can facilitate success in the general education curriculum and setting.

RECOMMENDED RESOURCES

Administrative Leadership in Inclusive Schools

Capper, C.A., & Frattura, E.M. (2009). *Meeting the needs of students of all abilities: How leaders go beyond inclusion* (2nd ed.). Thousand Oaks, CA: Corwin.

Marzano, R.J., Waters, T., & McNulty, B.A. (2005). *School leadership that works: From research to results.* Alexandria, VA: Association for Supervision and Curriculum Development.

McLaughlin, M.J., & Nolet, V. (2004). *What every principal needs to know about special education.* Thousand Oaks, CA: Corwin.

Stivers, J., Francis-Cropper, & Straus, M. (2008). Educating families about inclusive education: A month-by-month guide for teachers of inclusive classes. *Intervention in School and Clinic, 44*(1), 10–17.

Tomlinson, C.A., & Allan, S.D. (2000). *Leadership for differentiating schools & classrooms.* Alexandria, VA: Association for Supervision and Curriculum Development.

Villa, R.A., & Thousand, J.S. (Eds.) (2005). *Creating an inclusive school* (2nd ed.). Alexandria, VA: Association for Supervision and Curriculum Development.

Peer Friendships and Support

Best Buddies (http://www.bestbuddies.org)

California Department of Education (http://www.pubs.ca.gov/tcsii/ch12/lngmnortyprnt guard.aspx)

Carter, E.W., Cushing, L.S., & Kennedy, C.H. (2009). *Peer support strategies for improving all students' social lives and learning.* Baltimore: Paul H. Brookes Publishing Co.

The Center on School, Family, and Community Partnerships at Johns Hopkins University and the National Center for Culturally Responsive Educational Systems (http://www.nccrest .org)

Hughes, C., & Carter, E.W. (2008). *Peer buddy programs for successful secondary school inclusion.* Baltimore: Paul H. Brookes Publishing Co.

National Center for Parent Involvement in Education (http://www.ncpie.org)

National Network of Partnership Schools (http://www.csos.jhu/p2000/center.htm)

National Parent Teacher Association (http://www.pta.org)

Stivers, J., Francis-Cropper, & Straus, M. (2008). Educating families about inclusive education: A month-by-month guide for teachers of inclusive classes. *Intervention in School and Clinic, 44* (1), 10–17.

Parent Involvement

Epstein, J. (2001). *School, family, and community partnerships: Preparing educators and improving schools.* Boulder, CO: Westview Press.

REFERENCES

Barnett, C., & Monda-Amaya, L.E. (1998). Principals' knowledge of and attitudes toward inclusion. *Remedial and Special Education, 19*(3), 181–192.

Billingsley, B.S. (2005). *Cultivating and keeping committed special education teachers: What principals and district leaders can do.* Thousand Oaks, CA: Corwin.

Capper, C.A., & Frattura, E.M. (2009). *Meeting the needs of students of all abilities: How leaders go beyond inclusion* (2nd ed.). Thousand Oaks, CA: Corwin.

Carter, E.W., Cushing, L.S., Clark, N.M., & Kennedy, C.H. (2005). Effects of peer support interventions on students' access to the general curriculum and social interactions. *Research and Practice for Persons with Severe Disabilities, 30*(1), 15–25.

Carter, E.W., Cushing, L.S., & Kennedy, C.H. (2008, March/April). *Promoting rigor, relevance, and relationships through peer support interventions.* Washington, DC: The Association for Persons with Severe Handicaps.

Carter, E.W., & Kennedy, C.H. (2006). Promoting access to the general curriculum using peer support strategies. *Research and Practice for Persons with Severe Disabilities, 31,* 284–292.

Copeland, S.R., Hughes, C., Carter, E.W., Guth, C., Presley, J.A., Williams, C.R., & Fowler, S.E. (2004). Increasing access to general education: Perspectives of participants in a high school peer support program. *Remedial and Special Education, 25*(6), 342–352.

Copeland, S.R., McCall, J., Williams, C.R., Guth, C., Carter, E.W., Fowler, S.E., & Hughes, C. (2002). High school peer buddies: A win–win situation. *Teaching Exceptional Children, 35*(1), 16–21.

Cushing, L.S., & Kennedy, C.H. (1997). Academic effects on students without disabilities who serve as peer supports for students with disabilities in general education classrooms. *Journal of Applied Behavior Analysis, 30,* 139–152.

Epstein, J. (1995, May). School/family/community partnerships: Caring for children we share. *Phi Delta Kappan, 76*(9), 701–712.

Epstein, J., Sanders, M.G., Simons, B.S., Salinas, K.C., Jansorn, N.R., & Van Voorhis, F.L. (2002). *School, family, and community partnerships: Your handbook for action.* Thousand Oaks, CA: Corwin.

Giangreco, M.F., Edelman, S., Cloninger, C., & Dennis, R. (1993). My child has a classmate with severe disabilities: What parents of nondisabled children think about full inclusion. *Developmental Disabilities Bulletin, 21*(1), 77–91.

Guarino, C.M., Santibanez, L., & Daley, G.A. (2006). Teacher recruitment and retention: A review of the recent empirical literature. *Review of Educational Research, 76*(2), 173–208.

Henderson, A., & Berla, N. (1994). *A new generation of evidence: A family is critical to student achievement.* Washington, DC: Center for Law and Education.

Henderson, A., & Mapp, K. (2002). *A new wave of evidence: The impact of school, family and community connections on student achievement.* Austin, TX: Southwest Educational Development Laboratory.

Hughes, C., & Carter, E.W. (2008). *Peer buddy programs for successful secondary school inclusion.* Baltimore: Paul H. Brookes Publishing Co.

Hughes, C., Copeland, S.R., Guth, C., Rung, L.L., Hwang, B., Kleeb, G., et al. (2001). General education students' perspectives on their involvement in a high school peer buddy program. *Education and Training in Mental Retardation and Developmental Disabilities, 36*(3), 343–356.

Hughes, C., Guth, C., Hall, S., Presley, J., Dye, M., & Byers, C. (1999). They are my best friends: Peer buddies promote inclusion in high school. *Teaching Exceptional Children, 31*(5), 32–37.

Kennedy, C.H., & Itkonen, T. (1994). Some effects of regular class participation on the social contacts and social networks of high school students with severe disabilities. *Journal of the Association for Persons with Severe Handicaps, 19,* 1–10.

Marzano, R.J., Waters, T., & McNulty, B.A. (2005). *School leadership that works: From research to results.* Alexandria, VA: Association for Supervision and Curriculum Development.

McLaughlin, M.J., & Nolet, V. (2004). *What every principal needs to know about special education.* Thousand Oaks, CA: Corwin.

Michigan Department of Education. (2001). *What research says about parent involvement in children's education in relation to academic achievement.* Retrieved June 5, 2009, from http://www.mi.gov/documents/Final_Parent_Involvement_Fact_Sheet_14732_7.pdf

Michigan State University, University Outreach and Engagement Center. (2004, June). *Best practice briefs.* Retrieved June 5, 2009, from http://outreach.msu.edu/bpbriefs/issues/brief30.pdf

Nathan, J. (1996). *Benefits of parent and family involvement.* Retrieved June 2, 2009, from http://www.ncrel .org/sdrs/areas/issues/envrnmnt/famncomm/pa1lk37.htm

Palmer, D.S., Fuller, K., Arora, T., & Nelson, M. (2001). Taking sides: Parent views on inclusion for their children with severe disabilities. *Exceptional Children, 67,* 467–484.

Praisner, C.L. (2003). Attitudes of elementary school principles toward the inclusion of students with disabilities. *Exceptional Children, 69*(2), 135–145.

Reeves, D.B. (2006). *The learning leader: How to focus school improvement for better results.* Alexandria, VA: Association for Supervision and Curriculum Development.

Salend, S.J. (2006). Explaining your inclusion program to families. *Teaching Exceptional Children, 38*(4), 6–11.

Shukla, S., Kennedy, C.H., & Cushing, L.S. (1999). Intermediate school students with severe disabilities: Supporting their social participation in general education classrooms. *Journal of Positive Behavior Interventions, 1,* 130–140.

Speth, T., Saifer, S., & Forehand, G. (2008). *Parent involvement activities in school improvement plans in the Northwest region.* Washington, DC: Institute of Education Sciences, U.S. Department of Education.

Stivers, J., Francis-Cropper, L. & Straus, M. (2008). Educating families about inclusive education: A month-by-month guide for teachers of inclusive classes. *Intervention in School and Clinic, 44*(1), 10–17.

Thousand , J.S., & Villa, R.A. (2005). Organizational supports for change toward inclusive schooling. In R.A. Villa & J.S. Thousand (Eds.), *Creating an inclusive school* (2nd ed.). Alexandria, VA: Association for Supervision and Curriculum Development.

Tomlinson, C.A., & Allan, S.D. (2000). *Leadership for differentiating schools & classrooms.* Alexandria, VA: Association for Supervision and Curriculum Development.

Villa, R.A., & Thousand, J.S. (Eds.). (2005). *Creating an inclusive school* (2nd ed.). Alexandria, VA: Association for Supervision and Curriculum Development.

Leadership in the IEP Process
Going Beyond Procedural Compliance

School leaders' interests in the IEP process have traditionally (and understandably) been focused on procedural compliance with provisions of IDEA. Resources (including web sites and published materials) for IEP teams typically focus on legal requirements regarding timelines, content, and documentation, with much less attention to more qualitative aspects of the process. Despite recognition of the IEP as the backbone of special education services, less attention has been paid to how its implementation could enhance the experiences and outcomes for included learners. This chapter on the IEP process highlights several approaches, strategies, and procedures that have been recommended in the professional literature as effective practice and that have special relevance for included learners. The IEP process—which includes gathering information, planning, conducting the meeting, implementing the IEP provisions, and monitoring and reporting progress—is rich in opportunities for collaboration and is regarded as a foundation of inclusive education.

The IEP process has been the subject of very few research studies, partly because it is a legally mandated set of procedures with few elements open to experimentation. Concerns that attempts at innovation—even when effective—may increase the already substantial workload associated with the IEP process may also deter team members from pursuing new strategies. However, opportunities do exist for meeting and exceeding requirements, and recommended practices have been forwarded in the professional literature. In this chapter, we will discuss recommended practices that have the potential to enhance the benefits of the IEP process beyond what is legally required. The IEP enhancements presented in this chapter involve different elements of the IEP process. The probability of their use, with fidelity, requires leadership on the part of the special education administrator, principal, special educator, general educator(s), and remaining members of the IEP team, including the learner and parent.

The rationale for wanting to go beyond compliance in the IEP process can be heard in the excerpts from interviews with students, teachers, and parents—all of whom were asked a variation of the question, "When is the IEP process most helpful for an included learner, and when is it least helpful?"

Mr. T. (seventh-grade social studies teacher)

The best IEPs I have been involved in were the ones in which the special education teacher met with all of the general education teachers before the meeting to talk about how the student was doing in our classes. We had a chance to compare notes about the student and discuss ways we had been able to help the student be successful. When we got to the meeting, we were working with an accurate picture of the student and I felt that the IEP goals and the accommodations we agreed on were useful in the content area classes. Unfortunately, I have also been involved when there was minimal communication about the student ahead of time, and the opinion of the content area teachers did not seem important. In those cases, the goals and accommodations chosen did not always match what was happening in my classroom. Sometimes I'm not sure why I am there or how to help.

Sam (fourth-grade student with a learning disability)

I think it works best when I can get help in my classroom. Sometimes my teachers ask me how I am doing and what kind of help I need. Other times I don't say anything about my IEP, and sometimes don't even go to the meeting. I think that your IEP is not helpful if you don't get the help you need to do the work.

Mrs. M. (parent of a sixth-grade student with mild cognitive disability)

It is hard to explain the different experiences we have had with the IEP process. The basics are always the same, but what actually happens and how the team interacts can be completely different. The most productive IEPs have been those in which there was good communication between the special education and general education teachers, and there was a real attempt to choose goals and modifications that could be worked on within the general education classroom. The worst IEP experience was one where the general education teacher did not participate much, and afterward he seemed reluctant to work on the goals we had chosen. He even said that he did not think the IEP was "realistic" for his classroom. It seems as though we don't have a common vision in mind.

Ms. R. (special education teacher)

The IEP is most helpful when we get total cooperation from the general education teachers so that we are working as a team. When this happens, we end up with goals and accommodations that are relevant to what is happening in the classroom. We depend on the general education teachers to tell us what is expected in their classrooms so that we can anticipate problems. When there is a communication break-down, we sometimes end up choosing goals and supports that aren't supported by the classroom teacher. We also need the student to "buy-in" to his or her IEP, and to get this you have to have them involved in the process. More than once I have tried to do what was indicated in the IEP only to have the student say they weren't having that problem and did not need help. I would say that the IEP process is least helpful when it doesn't take into account what is actually happening in the classroom.

COMMON THEMES

The common themes in the above responses include full participation and investment by all team members; a shared understanding of the expectations in the general education classroom; and guidelines or a framework for determining goals and objectives and for choosing accommodations and modifications. We have encountered these concerns (and others) in our practice and in our research.

This chapter describes how critical elements in the IEP process can be enhanced to increase the likelihood of learner success. The critical enhancements we address include maximizing participation by general educators, aligning goals and objectives with the general curriculum, monitoring progress in the general education classroom, strategically balancing accommodations and modifications, and maximizing student involvement in their IEP process. To understand why these enhancements have emerged over the past decade, we first review how IDEA has influenced the IEP process and created expanded roles for general education.

IDEA GUIDELINES AND THE IEP

The IDEA Amendments of 1997 (PL 105-17) created an explicit link between the IEP and the general education curriculum through the following requirements:

1. Participation of a general education teacher in the IEP meeting

2. A statement of the child's present level of performance (academic and functional performance)

3. An explanation of the extent to which the child will not participate with other children in the general classroom

4. An expectation that the learner will participate in statewide and districtwide assessment, with appropriate accommodations as determined by the IEP team

IDEA 2004 (PL 108-446) continued the above provisions and emphasized access to the general curriculum within a general education classroom (Ahearn, 2006). Together, the above guidelines are intended to maintain the IEP team's focus on the general education curriculum as the framework for curricular and instructional decisions for learners with disabilities. A 1999 survey of state special education administrators revealed that the 1997 provisions had resulted in positive changes in IEP process, including shared understanding by special and general educators (Project FORUM, National Association for State Directors of Special Education [NASDSE], 1999).

In a series of research studies in the late 1990s, concerns were raised about the extent to which IEPs for included learners may focus more on the expectations of the general education curriculum at the expense of individualized goals and specialized instruction, which reflect the needs of the specific learner and the overarching mission of special education (Baker & Zigmond, 1995; Espin, Deno, & Albayrak-Kaymak, 1998; Zigmond & Baker, 1995). This research served as a caution that the assumption that simply including learners in the general education classroom and basing IEP goals on learning standards would translate into progress on the general curriculum. Our obligation to provide specialized, individualized instruction is not forfeited, even when coordination becomes more complex. Leaders in the IEP process must remain cognizant of the challenging balance between a focus on the expectations of the general curriculum and setting and individual learning needs, and between specialized instruction and accommodations.

In the next section, we discuss how each of the enhancements cited previously can be improved through implementation of strategies described in the professional literature or field tested in our own experiences.

Enhancement: Maximizing General Educator Participation

IDEA requires participation of a general educator in the IEP, but it does not specify a particular role to be played or what is expected of a general educator in the IEP process. The importance of participation throughout the IEP process—not just at the meeting—has not been fully recognized (Project FORUM, NASDSE, 1998) and the contribution of general educators to the process can vary significantly among teams. General educators motivated to support an included learner are still in need of knowledge of how and when to contribute to the IEP process.

The relatively small body of research involving the IEP process includes little attention to the participation of general educators in the process. In a study of perceptions of the IEP process (Lee-Tarver, 2006), general educators indicated that they use their students' IEPs to plan instruction (specifically to make decisions regarding the sequencing of curriculum and instruction) and to evaluate progress on learning objectives. Such research suggests that general educators do see value in the IEP process and the resulting document, and that efforts to enhance their participation in the process may be valued and productive.

Our experience suggests that the way in which general educators approach and participate in the IEP process significantly affects the quality of the resulting program and how it is implemented and monitored. General educators bring knowledge and experience that, when transmitted to the team, provides a reference point for selecting goals and objectives, as well as determining what accommodations, modifications, or specialized instruction will best serve the learner in the classroom. Box 4.1 presents the type of information the general educator transmits to the IEP team. As indicated, information regarding the types of resources available to all students is important when determining what accommodations or modifications might be necessary for an individual learner.

Box 4.1. ★ Information transmitted by the general educator to the IEP team

1. The curricular expectations for all learners, including specific learning standards or goals
2. The types of instructional approaches (e.g., lecture, small-group projects) used and the extent to which differentiation (e.g., students choose from a menu of options) is already incorporated into instructional design for a specific class or content area
3. The types of assessments (e.g., in-class tests, quizzes, poster presentations) used in the classroom to measure students' progress
4. Study resources (e.g., online study guides, individual meetings with the teacher, peer tutoring) available for all learners who struggle learning the content
5. The level of independence (e.g., students expected to monitor their homework completion) and self-determination (e.g., students expected to ask for help when needed) expected of all students
6. The types of individualized supports or accommodations (e.g., extra time on assignments, guided notes) that have proven effective for learners in the past
7. The extent to which instruction is delivered with technology and how learners use technology in their daily classwork

Box 4.2. ★ Guiding questions for general educators with an included learner

1. How has the learner performed on the class curriculum?
   ★ Evidence includes work products, test scores, and grades.
2. On which types of assignments is the learner most successful?
   ★ Compare performance on different types of assignments and grading elements.
3. What types of assignments seem to interact most with the learner's exceptionality to cause lower achievement and/or or a greater need for accommodation?
   ★ Compare performance on assignments that require the learner to use skills and abilities most affected by his or her exceptionality (e.g., reading comprehension, abstract thinking) and those that allow the learner to rely on strengths.
4. How and when are accommodations made for the learner?
5. How and when are modifications made for the learner?
6. How and when is extra support provided for the learner?
   ★ Consider both formal (e.g., after-school tutoring) and informal (e.g., getting help from peers during groupwork) support.
7. How and when does the learner ask for help?
8. Does the learner exhibit behavior that interferes with learning in the classroom?
9. How successful is the learner in interacting with peers and forming friendships?
10. Which IEP goals are addressed in your class? How are they addressed?
11. How is progress on IEP goals measured in your class?

General educators also transmit information regarding learners included in their classrooms. The type and specificity of what is reported in the IEP process can affect the outcome positively or negatively. Box 4.2 lists guiding questions that general educators should consider when preparing to discuss the performance of a learner in their class.

LEADERSHIP AND THE STAR ORGANIZER

The STAR organizer (Table 4.1) presents leadership activities for maximizing general educator participation in the IEP process. Administrators should focus on establishing a schoolwide perception of the IEP process as a shared responsibility of the general educators, special educators, and related services personnel. Shared responsibility requires communication and collaboration. Both of these require time to meet face to face; hence, they may require scheduling changes and creative efforts to free up time. Articulating an IEP process that includes explicit participation by the general educator is recommended, as are development or adoption of organizers to guide team members in preparing for the IEP meeting. Valuing, seeking, and guiding participation by the general educator is everyone's responsibility.

Enhancement: Aligning the IEP with the General Curriculum

The term *access to the general curriculum* has been used in the professional literature to describe an overarching approach to the design of special education services and supports that is intended to maximize exposure to, participation in, and mastery of the general curriculum

STAR ORGANIZER

MAXIMIZING GENERAL EDUCATOR PARTICIPATION IN THE IEP PROCESS

Table 4.1.

AREA OF PRACTICE	SAMPLE LEADERSHIP ACTIVITIES
Setting the tone	• Use faculty meetings to establish a vision for teacher involvement in the IEP process; include this vision in school documents such as the parent/student handbook. • Principals and team leaders maximize involvement in IEP meetings and take a lead with ideas to support inclusive decisions. • Arrange for substitutes for release time for teams to prepare in advance for complex IEP meetings.
 *Translating research into practice*	• Follow the general guidelines in Chapter 2 (Table 2.3) for identifying, implementing, and evaluating new practices. • Review research on effective teaming and collaboration among general and special educators and create organizers and tools for use in the IEP process. • Create tools and organizers to guide general educators in the IEP process. • Develop a standard protocol for classroom teacher participation in IEP meetings.
 **Arranging for collaboration**	• Establish teacher articulation meetings at the start of each school year to discuss individual student IEPs and classroom supports needed. • Schedule shared plan time each week for general and special education staff. • Ensure that a system is in place for teachers to share successful inclusive strategies for individual students as they move to the next grade.
 *Reflecting on processes and outcomes*	• Principals and special education administrators should confer periodically on whether changes are needed in the quality of general education participation in the IEP process. • Solicit parent feedback on the IEP process in your school (see Chapter 6).

(Nolet & McLaughlin, 2005). General strategies for increasing access are discussed in Chapter 5; here we focus on implications for the IEP process. Emphasis on increasing access to the general education curriculum is a result of NCLB and IDEA requirements that learners with special needs participate in large-scale assessments. A focus on access provides other potential benefits, including that of a guiding principle or framework for developing IEPs that promote success in the general education classroom.

Along with the implementation of large-scale accountability measures, efforts were made to standardize expectations through a common set of standards for all learners. Readers may be familiar with terms such as *standards-based reform* and likely have experience with aligning their own curriculum and instruction with their state's standards and accountability measures. Standards-based reform has potential benefits for learners with special needs because schools must monitor their achievement and implement strategies to address performance problems (Thurlow, 2002). Higher expectations resulting from a focus on standards have led to improved achievement for learners with special needs (Nolet & McLaughlin, 2005). Recognizing that learning standards reflect the goal of general education instruction, many IEP teams now conceptualize the IEP as a means to promote progress toward meeting state and national learning standards. Terms such as *standards-based IEP* and *standards-linked IEP* denote IEPs that include goals and objectives influenced by learning standards.

Cortiella (2008) has suggested that students benefit from a standards-based approach to IEP development because they receive specially designed instruction linked to the general education curriculum for their grade level, appropriate accommodations designed to support achievement at grade level, and better preparation to earn a regular high school diploma and enjoy success beyond secondary school. A 2006 survey of state special education directors revealed both benefits and perceived limitations of standards-based IEPs (Ahearn, 2006). Perceived benefits included increased focus of instruction delivered by special educators on general education curriculum and a reduction in the use of a separate curriculum. Major concerns included the lack of staff training in implementation of standards-based IEPs and a tendency for staff turnover to negatively affect consistent practice. These concerns reflect a need for leadership in preparing teams and establishing systems that will outlive any one individual's participation.

The link between learning standards and IEP goals has been achieved by adopting an actual learning standard (or substandard/indicator) as the goal. When a learner is working below grade level, a lower (modified) standard may serve as the IEP goal. In some cases, the

Illinois State Learning Standard:	
English Language Arts (late elementary, 3.B.2a): Generate and organize ideas using a variety of planning strategies (e.g., mapping, outlining, drafting).	
Strategy: Adopt actual learning standard for learner's grade level as goal.	**Goal:** Learner will generate and organize ideas using a variety of planning strategies (e.g., mapping, outlining, drafting).
Strategy: Adopt a modified (lower) learning standard when learner is working below grade level. In this example, the standard for early elementary learner may be appropriate.	**Goal:** (3.B.1a) Learner will use prewriting strategies to generate and organize ideas (e.g., focus on one topic; organize writing; use descriptive words).

Figure 4.1. Examples of linking standards and individualized education program goals. (*Source:* Illinois State Board of Education, 1997).

Step 1: Consider the grade-level content standards for the grade in which the learner is enrolled or would be enrolled based on age

Sample guiding question:

1. What is the standard saying the student must know and be able to do?

Step 2: Examine classroom and student data to determine where the student is functioning in relation to the grade-level standards

Sample guiding questions:

1. Has student been taught content aligned with grade-level standards?
2. What types of supports has student received to attain grade-level expectations?

Step 3: Develop the present level of academic achievement and functional performance

Sample guiding questions:

1. What are the student's strengths and needs in relation to accessing the general curriculum?
2. What assessment data can we use to establish how well the student is performing in the general curriculum?

Step 4: Develop measurable annual goals aligned with grade-level academic achievement

Sample guiding questions:

1. What can the student reasonably be expected to achieve in 1 year?
2. What are the student's needs as identified in the present level of performance?

Step 5: Assess and report the student's progress throughout the year

Sample guiding questions:

1. What types of assessments will we use to monitor progress?
2. How will progress be reported to parents?

Step 6: Identify specially designed instruction including accommodations and/or modifications needed to access and progress in the general curriculum

Sample guiding questions:

1. What accommodations have proven effective in the past?
2. What accommodations are needed to maximize access to the grade-level curriculum?

Step 7: Determine the most appropriate assessment option

Sample guiding questions:

1. What types of state assessments are available?
2. What types of accommodations are allowed?

Figure 4.2.   Seven-step process to creating standards-based individualized education programs. (From Holbrook, M.D. [2007]. *A seven-step process to creating standards-based IEPs.* Available on the Project FORUM, National Association of State Directors of Special Education web site: http://www.projectforum.org; reprinted by permission.)

goal is considered to be "standards referenced" in that it is not based directly on a standard, but does address a skill or strategy that the learner must use to progress toward the goal. Figure 4.1 presents an example of the ways in which standards influence IEP goals. Decisions about whether learning standards should be adopted as IEP goals are often based on whether the standards are written in a format that make sense as a goal.

Table 4.2. Standards-based individualized education program goal in reading for a learner with significant needs

Content area	Standard	Critical function	Objective
Language arts/ reading, Grade 6	Reading a variety of texts: The student reads widely for different purposes in varied sources.	Use of receptive communication (reading, listening, photographs, and drawings) for different purposes	*Presymbolic level:* The student activates a switch to listen to books on tape to read a book of her choice for pleasure, read a recipe that is used for a class project, read directions for walking to a different part of school, and read the next step in her personal daily schedule. *Early symbolic level:* The student orally reads pictured symbols to make a choice for her daily leisure activity, follow the next step in her daily schedule, follow pictured classroom rules, follow instructions for classroom arts and crafts activities, and use a communication board to interact with peers. *Expanded symbolic level:* The student reads basic instructions within multiple contexts to follow directions to microwave a dinner of her choice, prepare a cake mix, follow instructions from in-building signs, obtain items on a grocery list, and find items in a catalog.

From Lynch, S., & Adams, P. (2008). Developing standards-based individualized education program objectives for students with significant needs. *Teaching Exceptional Children, 40*(3). Reprinted with permission, copyright © 2008 by the Council for Exceptional Children, Inc. www.cec.sped.org. All rights reserved.

The process for standards-based IEPs resembles that commonly used by teams, with the addition of reference to learning standards in multiple steps. Figure 4.2 presents a process for creating standards-based IEPs.

Standards-based IEPs are also recommended for learners with more significant special needs, with special considerations in their development. Lynch and Adams (2008) outlined a process that includes the following elements unique to learners with significant special needs:

1. When determining the present level of performance, the team must attend to the learner's functional and academic performance.

2. When considering the critical functions of the relevant standards, the team must also consider the learner's adaptive skill and symbolic level (i.e., the extent to which the learner recognizes and uses conventional symbols, such as words and numbers).

An example of a standards-based IEP goal for a learner with significant special needs is presented in Table 4.2.

As we indicated earlier, IEP goals must consider the demands of the general education curriculum in the context of the unique needs of the individual learner. Too much emphasis on meeting general education standards at the expense of individual needs in academics (e.g., reading fluency), functional skills (e.g., organizing work), or adaptive social behavior (e.g., minimizing disruptive behavior) will not address the learner's needs and will undermine progress. Maximizing input from all team members is the best strategy for reaching an ideal balance in standards-based IEPs.

Teams must be fully informed of applicable learning standards before alignment of IEPs can occur—a task that requires professional development and ongoing communication, and thus involves leadership by administrators and team members. Once steps are taken to ensure that everyone is familiar with applicable standards, the next step involves articulating a process for linking the IEP goals and objectives in academic areas. Leadership will be evidenced

Table 4.3.

STAR ORGANIZER
FOR ALIGNING THE IEP WITH THE GENERAL CURRICULUM

AREA OF PRACTICE	SAMPLE LEADERSHIP ACTIVITIES
Setting the tone	• Hold brief data retreats during faculty meetings to review the performance of students with IEPs relative to adequate yearly progress standards. • Principals and special education administrators should collaborate to ensure that all teachers understand IEP legal requirements and best practice in providing access to knowledge in the general curriculum.
 *Translating research into practice*	• Follow the general guidelines in Chapter 2 (Table 2.3) for identifying, implementing, and evaluating new practices. • Review and share a process for creating standards-based IEPs. • Design professional development activities on writing measurable, standards-based IEPs.
 *Arranging for collaboration*	• Establish summer curriculum projects for general and special educators and other education staff (e.g., paraprofessionals) to develop curriculum modifications and assessments needed for target content areas (e.g., science, social studies) for the upcoming year (and save materials for repeated use). • Ensure that special educators participate on curriculum committees and subject area articulation meetings. • Communicate information regarding learning standards and their integration into the IEP process to students and parents; provide resources to prepare students and parents for implementing standards-based IEPs.
 *Reflecting on processes and outcomes*	• Administrators should examine sample IEPs to assess alignment of goals to curriculum, and whether accommodations and modifications are tailored to the needs of individual students. • Solicit feedback from students, parents, and teams regarding the strengths and limitations of the process for implementing standards-based IEPs.

when all team members understand the process and expectations, and IEPs reflect consistent linkage to standards blended with the unique needs of each individual learner. Table 4.3 presents sample leadership activities for the STAR organizer.

Enhancement: Monitoring Progress in the General Curriculum

The ways in which learner progress on IEP goals and objectives is assessed directly affect the quality of information, which teams must rely on to make important decisions regarding how to instruct and support. Data on student progress is also vital when making the larger decision of whether the learner is making progress in the general education classroom—an indicator of the least restrictive environment. Data collected in monitoring progress on IEP goals serve as the baseline for the next generation of goals and objectives. Data therefore directly influence how the team evaluates whether a learner is making progress in the general education classroom and whether the current supports (e.g., accommodations) are adequate (Capizzi, 2008).

Many IEP forms require only that the team designate the type of assessment method (e.g., classroom work) and the frequency of reporting (e.g., monthly). Therefore, opportunities for collaboration and shared ownership of progress monitoring go unfulfilled. Careful planning must go into progress monitoring for included learners. It may be necessary to allow for individualized assessments or projects to display progress by a student if the IEP team believes that there are not enough opportunities to track progress. Failure to plan and regularly collect data can leave an IEP team in the difficult and uncomfortable situation of having to make decisions based on memory and judgment rather than tangible evidence.

Progress on IEP goals and objectives can be assessed through different types of measures. When used in combination, they provide the most accurate picture of the learner's success in the general education classroom. Direct measures involve the recording of actual student performance, such as curriculum-based assessments based on the classroom curricula, standardized curriculum-based measures (e.g., the Dynamic Indicators of Basic Early Literacy Skills [DIBELS] for beginning reading ability), or observational data of the learner's behavior in the classroom. Direct measures are inherently valid in that they reflect actual performance; limitations to their use are usually related to the resources needed for administration. Schools that are implementing response-to-intervention (RTI) models will likely be using some type of standardized or curriculum-based measure that can serve as one direct measure for progress monitoring. Indirect measures include rubrics that provide a holistic rating of learner performance and self-evaluation instruments that are completed by the student. Informal measures involve applying criteria to the evaluation of work products or performances; their validity hence relies on teachers and students using the measures with fidelity. An advantage of indirect measures is that they are generally easy to implement and may be used with assignments generated in the flow of classroom instruction. Involving learners in monitoring their progress may facilitate a sense of personal accountability and self-determination.

A third type of measure—authentic—may include portfolio, videotaped performances, or other individualized forms of assessment designed to capture progress. Authentic assessments are often used to complement traditional assessments by providing detailed examples of student achievement (Etscheidt, 2006). Teams must determine a combination of measures to provide a valid picture of the learner's performance, and develop a plan for the systematic collection of performance data. Figure 4.3 is a tool that can be used by teams to plan for effective progress monitoring.

Leadership in monitoring progress is evidenced when teams develop a plan for monitoring progress for each IEP. The plan reflects shared responsibility among team members. A clearly articulated IEP process and the availability of tools and organizers to guide planning

IEP goal/ objective	Criteria for completion	Types of measures	Who will collect data?	When and where will data be collected?	Who will summarize and report data?
		Direct			
		Indirect			
		Authentic			

Figure 4.3. Planning organizer for progress monitoring.

are logical places to begin building consistent practice. Sample leadership activities for monitoring progress in the general education curriculum are presented in Table 4.4.

Enhancement: Strategically Balancing Accommodations and Modifications

Although accommodations and modifications are well-established practices for learners with special needs, considerable confusion still exists among IEP teams regarding differences and implications of these supports. Such confusion may be caused by the fact that the terms are used interchangeably and may be blended together into a checklist within the IEP document. Leadership is needed to ensure that all IEP team members, including parents, understand the different purposes and implications for accommodations and modifications. Table 4.5 presents examples of what all team members should know.

Modifications can be considered to have an inverse relationship with the general curriculum: As the degree of modification increases, time spent in the general curriculum decreases (Nolet & McLaughlin, 2005). For learners with moderate to significant special needs, modifications to the content and instruction in the general education classroom may be appropriate. Students with significant needs are also more likely to participate in alternative assessments based on alternate achievement standards. However, for learners with milder special needs, modifications should be used strategically after the IEP team has determined that all appropriate accommodations have been provided and all other types of supports (e.g., tutoring) have been exhausted. In our experience, teams that have a shared understanding of benefits and implications are better prepared to choose accommodations and modifications strategically.

Because accommodations and modifications have been recommended for included students for more than two decades, most team members will be familiar with more popular strategies (e.g., extra time). Furthermore, most teams seek to streamline the IEP process, including the meeting, by creating tools that commonly present accommodations and modifications intermixed in a checklist format. Thus, leaders may need to encourage teams to step

STAR ORGANIZER
FOR MONITORING PROGRESS IN THE GENERAL EDUCATION CURRICULUM

Table 4.4.

AREA OF PRACTICE	SAMPLE LEADERSHIP ACTIVITIES
 **Setting the tone**	• Emphasize shared responsibility for monitoring progress in the regular education classroom. • Review current data on the percentage of students with disabilities currently meeting grade-level targets on universal screening tools. • Use team/department meetings to set annual goals for increasing the performance of IEP students.
 **Translating research into practice**	• Follow the general guidelines in Chapter 2 (Table 2.3) for identifying, implementing, and evaluating new practices. • Review and share evidence-based procedures for effective screening and progress monitoring for all students, including those with special needs (see http://www.student progress.org).

 **Arranging for collaboration**	• Organize problem-solving teams to review ongoing assessment data at each tier of instruction.
	  o School improvement team: Tier 1
	  o Grade/department teams: Tier 2
	  o Individual problem solving: Tier 3

 **Reflecting on processes and outcomes**	• Schedule data sessions three or four times per year. • Ask each team to report on data at each tier for all students, including students with disabilities.

back and think more carefully about how they are using accommodations and modifications strategically to allow students to progress in the general education curriculum and setting. Leadership in this area will involve ensuring that all team members, including parents, understand the information provided in Table 4.5. This may be achieved through professional development, as well as tools for guiding the team through effective decision making regarding balancing of accommodations, modifications, and specialized instruction. The STAR organizer for strategically balancing accommodations and modifications is presented in Table 4.6.

Table 4.5. What all team members should know about accommodations and modifications

	Accommodations	Modification
Purpose	• Reduce or minimize the interaction of a student's learning differences with the classroom demands. • Allow a valid assessment of content learned that is not affected by the presence of a learning difference.	• Working with a lower learning standard or goal appropriate to ability level • May involve working on less content, or parallel content at lower grade level
Examples	• Extra time to complete tests • Speech-to-text software for writing assignments • Audio texts to supplement print texts • Able to respond orally for some written assignments	• Expected to master 3–10 concepts in science class • Working on addition and subtraction while class works on multiplication and division
Effect on grading	• Should not result in reduced expectations • Should not require a different grading system	• Usually requires an individualized grading system based on lower standards or goals • Should be documented in the individualized education program and reports to parents must indicate grades based on individualized goals
Potential implications for diploma and post-secondary applications	• Should not impact points or credits toward graduation • Should not influence application to post-secondary institutions	• Could affect access to certain college classes if prerequisites not met • Could require special/alternative diploma, which could affect postsecondary options

Enhancement: Maximizing Student Involvement in the IEP Process

Our last enhancement involves maximizing the student's participation in his or her IEP, often cited as a rich opportunity to promote self-determination. Research has suggested that important benefits are associated with teaching learners to engage in self-determination in their educational programs and their after-school lives (Wehmeyer & Palmer, 2003; Wehmeyer & Schwartz, 1997). Self-determination skills include clarifying preferences, making choices, self-evaluating performance, and advocating for oneself. The IEP process provides ample opportunity for learners to acquire, practice, and use a broad range of important skills that can be generalized to other contexts. Furthermore, learners who actively participate in their IEP process are more motivated to follow through on its provisions and to interact with teachers and parents about the IEP on an ongoing basis. Research to date suggests that learners are not being prepared and encouraged to participate more fully in their IEP process even though they may be learning related self-determination skills (e.g., making choices) as part of their educational program (Agran & Hughes, 2008). Based on our experience, in schools where leadership focused on inclusiveness has emerged, the practice of greater student participation in planning and choice making has emerged. These leaders understand how the IEP process can be enhanced to improve satisfaction and increase achievement.

We perceive an additional benefit to maximizing involvement by included learners, particularly those in middle and high school, because only the students can report their "lived experience" in the general classroom. Although teachers and parents can share work products and observations, students can describe how they have learned best in a class, as well as the types of supports that are most and least helpful. Learner attitudes toward individual-

STAR ORGANIZER
Table 4.6.
FOR STRATEGICALLY BALANCING ACCOMMODATIONS AND MODIFICATIONS

AREA OF PRACTICE	SAMPLE LEADERSHIP ACTIVITIES
 **Setting the tone**	• Conduct principal-facilitated open faculty discussion to establish shared beliefs regarding "fairness" in balancing high standards with individual student needs. • Meet with grade-level/department teams to discuss procedures for grading when students require extensive accommodations or modifications.
 **Translating research into practice**	• Follow the general guidelines in Chapter 2 (Table 2.3) for identifying, implementing, and evaluating new practices. • Provide professional development to clarify the purpose of and distinction between accommodations and modifications. • Create tools to guide planning for progress monitoring using multiple measures.
 **Arranging for collaboration**	• Provide opportunities for staff and parents to collaborate in advance of IEP meetings to propose possible accommodations or modifications, especially for more complex student profiles.
 **Reflecting on processes and outcomes**	• Engage teams in periodic discussion of adjustments that may be needed in the current school procedures for determining accommodations and modifications.

ized instruction and support change with maturity; failure to solicit their input often leads to selection of goals and supports not preferred by the learner, and hence they are less likely to be fully utilized. Unfortunately, research on IEP meetings has suggested that both learners and general educators are often marginalized in meetings dominated by administrators and the special educator (Martin, Marshall, & Sale, 2004). The STAR organizer for maximizing student involvement in the IEP process is presented in Table 4.7.

Models, curricula, and strategies for preparing learners to more fully participate in their IEP processes have been described in the professional literature. The self-directed IEP (Martin, Marshall, Maxson, & Jerman, 1997) is described in a published training program that includes structured lessons for teaching students to implement an 11-step process for leading their IEP

STAR ORGANIZER
FOR MAXIMIZING STUDENT INVOLVEMENT IN THE IEP PROCESS

Table 4.7.

AREA OF PRACTICE	SAMPLE LEADERSHIP ACTIVITIES
 **Setting the tone**	• Organize an advisory team of teachers, students, and parents to discuss guidelines for student participation in IEP meetings. • Include guidelines in student/parent handbooks and other school information sources.
Translating research into practice	• Follow the general guidelines in Chapter 2 (Table 2.3) for identifying, implementing, and evaluating new practices. • Review and share research that highlights best practice for preparing students for meaningful participation in the IEP process. • Adopt a program for preparing learners to lead their IEP processes.
Arranging for collaboration	• Ask the advisory team to create a menu of options to maximize comfort level and success for students as they participate in the IEP process. • Create opportunities for team members to work with the learner on their IEP process.
 **Reflecting on processes and outcomes**	• Ask IEP participants (including parents and students) to complete a quick "exit survey" following each IEP meeting. • Use this as a data source for discussing needed revisions in the IEP meeting process (see Tool 6.8 on page 118).

meeting. The program also includes tools from the *ChoiceMaker Self-Determination Curriculum* (Martin & Marshall, 1995) to guide the learner through preparation for the meeting, as well as a student workbook and instructional video. Research on the effectiveness of the self-directed IEP has suggested that learners completing the program are more likely to attend their meetings, better prepared to lead their meetings and contribute during the meeting, able to create better goal statements, and have more positive perceptions of their IEPs (Allen, Smith, Test, Flowers, & Wood, 2001; Martin et al., 2006; Snyder & Shapiro, 1997; Snyder, 2002). In addition, Martin et al. (2006) found that student-led IEPs did not take longer than those led by staff, thereby dispelling one concern for busy administrators and teachers. Information regarding the *ChoiceMaker Self-Determination Curriculum* and the self-directed IEP can be found at http://www.sopriswest.com.

Student-Led IEPs: A Guide for Student Involvement (McGahee, Mason, Wallace, & Jones, 2001) guides the learner and his or her teachers through the process of preparing for and leading their IEP meeting. Research suggests that the guide is effective for preparing learners to participate more effectively in the IEP process. General educators perceived students as having a better understanding of their rights and needs, as well as how to utilize resources (Mason, McGahee-Kovac, & Johnson, 2004; Mason, McGahee-Kovac, Johnson, & Stillerman, 2002). Figure 4.4 presents an example of a tool used to guide the learner in preparing for the IEP meeting.

Obviously, preparing learners to participate more fully in their IEP processes takes time and resources; flexibility and creativity are helpful, too. Barrie and McDonald (2002) presented an administrator's experience in which instruction on key skills was integrated into several courses, including general education, and a partnership with outside advocacy agencies and a university provided additional staff to conduct training sessions. Some schools deliver the necessary instruction and practice during after-school sessions, resource or study periods, or a self-advocacy course that high school students can take for credit.

An additional approach to preparing learners for participation involves instruction on strategies designed to prompt the learner through critical steps in the process. Strategies include a mnemonic device to help the learner remember each step in the process, thereby reducing reliance on adult supervision. Figure 4.5 presents an example of a strategy that has been used to increase student participation in their IEP meetings. Teaching learners to use a strategy to lead their IEPs involves a sequence of modeling, guided practice, and independent practice; thus, instructional time must be scheduled. Learners may benefit from the presence of a visual reminder of the steps in their strategy as they progress toward independence.

Konrad (2008) has described a 20-step process for involving learners in the IEP process that describes multiple goals related to developing background knowledge, planning for the

---

My Strengths and Needs

My name: _____   Date: _____

Class: _____   Teacher: _____

What do I do well?

What helps me do my best?

What do I need to do even better?

Figure 4.4.   Example of tool on student-led individualized education programs. (From McGahee, M., Mason, C., Wallace, T., & Jones, B. [2001]. *Student-led IEPs: A guide for student involvement.* Arlington, VA: Council for Exceptional Children; p. 21; reprinted with permission, copyright © 2001 by the Council for Exceptional Children, Inc. www.cec.sped.org. All rights reserved.)

```
                                  IPLAN

I   Inventory your learning strengths, areas to improve or learn, goals, choices for learning or
    accommodations
P   Provide your inventory information
L   Listen and respond
A   Ask questions
N   Name your goals

Examples of Probe Questions for Step 1 in IPLAN:
    What do you think are your strongest/weakest study or learning skills?
    What skills do you want to improve or learn that will help you do better in school?
    Are there after-school activities—such as sports, jobs, or clubs—in which you want to become
        involved?
    What types of study or learning activities work best for you?
```

Figure 4.5. Example of a strategy that increases learner participation. (*Sources:* Hammer [2004]; VanReusen, Deshler, & Schumaker [1984].)

IEP, drafting the IEP, meeting to develop the IEP, and implementing the IEP. Teams may find this process useful because it describes what should happen in each stage, and suggests how and when published materials may be best used.

Administrative leadership is critical for committing resources for implementation of student-led IEPs. Adequate preparation will require time for students to undergo training and practice under the guidance of school personnel. Leadership for preparing the learners can be distributed among team members. Perhaps most important is making clear the importance of supporting learners as they develop and use self-determination skills.

Preventing or Resolving Conflict with IEP Facilitation

The use of externally facilitated IEPs is emerging as a strategy for ensuring that the team remains focused on students and productively working toward an IEP that is satisfactory to everyone. IEP facilitation is not mediation and is not required by IDEA. However, many states now support school districts in providing IEP facilitation for cases in which conflict and ineffective communication may have undermined the ability of the team to work toward a satisfactory IEP.

IEP facilitation is not intended to focus specifically on issues related to inclusion; however, the fact that successful inclusion requires coordination of a complex set of supports means that advocacy, problem solving, and negotiation are vital in many cases. Effective leaders can often guide the IEP team through difficult meetings, but in those cases where no approach has proven effective, an external facilitator may be a solution. Information on IEP facilitation is available elsewhere from the Consortium for Appropriate Dispute Resolution in Special Education (http://www.directionservice.org/cadre) or the Technical Assistance Alliance for Parent Centers (http://www.taalliance.org).

WRAPPING UP AND LOOKING AHEAD

We discussed five strategies for enhancing your IEP processes beyond procedural compliance. These enhancements were chosen because they produce a clearer picture of a learner's experience in the general education classroom, and therefore allow the IEP team to make more informed decisions. Maximizing participation by the general educator and allowing students to lead their own IEPs are enhancements that reflect our evolved understanding of the limitations of a process dominated by administrators and the special educator. Implementing standards-based IEPs and balancing accommodations and modifications are enhancements to the structure and content of learners' IEPs, whereas progress monitoring addresses both the content and implementation of the IEP. Although distinct, all share the potential to bring clarity to the experience of the included learner.

In Chapter 5, we move from something unique to special education back to topics that are important to all learners; we explore large-scale initiatives that serve as background for implementing IEPs. Emphasis on maximizing access to the general curriculum, implementing universal design for learning, and assessing students' response to intervention are evolving approaches to maximizing the success of all learners, including those receiving special education services.

RECOMMENDED RESOURCES

Administrative Leadership in Inclusive Education

Bateman, D., & Bateman, C.F. (2006). *A principal's guide to special education* (2nd ed.). Arlington, VA: Council for Exceptional Children.

Center on Personnel Studies in Special Education (http://www.personnelcenter.org/pdf/copsse_principals.pdf)

Villa, R.A., & Thousand, J.S. (2005). *Creating an inclusive school* (2nd ed.). Alexandria, VA: Association for Supervision and Curriculum Development.

Wakeman, S.Y., Browder, D.M., Flowers, C., & Ahlgrim-Delzell, L. (2006). Principal's knowledge of fundamental and current issues in special education. *NASSP Bulletin, 90*(2), 153–174.

General Information on IDEA 2004 and IEP Guidelines

Bateman, B.D., & Linden, M.A. (2005). *Better IEPs: How to develop legally correct and educationally useful programs* (4th ed.). Verona, WI: IEP Resources.

Council for Exceptional Children. (2007). *Understanding IDEA 2004: Frequently asked questions.* Arlington, VA: Author.

Gartin, B.C., & Murdick, N.L. (2005). IDEA 2004: The IEP. *Intervention in School and Clinic, 26*(6), 327–331.

IDEA 2004, LD Online (http://www.ldonline.org/features/idea2004)

U.S. Department of Education (http://www.idea.ed.gov)

Wrightslaw (http://www.wrightslaw.com/idea/law.htm)

Standards-Based Reform and IEPs

Ahearn, E. (2006). *Standards-based IEPs: Implementation in selected states.* Alexandria, VA: Project Forum of the National Association of State Directors of Special Education.

Miller, L., & Hoffman, L. (2002). *Linking IEPs to state learning standards. A step-by-step guide.* Austin, TX: PRO-ED.

National Center for Learning Disabilities (http://www.ncld.org)

Nolet, V., & McLaughlin, M.J. (2005). *Accessing the general curriculum: Including students with disabilities in standards-based reform* (2nd ed.). Thousand Oaks, CA: Corwin.

Project FORUM, National Association of State Directors of Special Education (NASDSE) (http://www.projectforum.org)

Thurlow, M.L. (2002). Positive educational results: The promise of standards-based reform. *Remedial and Special Education, 23*(4), 195–202.

U.S. Department of Education (http://www.idea.ed.gov)

Monitoring Progress on the IEP and General Curriculum

Circle of Inclusion Project, University of Kansas (http://www.circleofinclusion.org)

Elliott, S.N., Braden, J.P., & White, J.L. (2001). *Assessing one and all: Educational accountability for students with disabilities.* Arlington, VA: Council for Exceptional Children.

Etscheidt, S.K. (2006). Progress monitoring: Legal issues and recommendations for IEP teams. *Teaching Exceptional Children, 38*(3), 56–60.

Florida Center for Reading Research, Progress Monitoring and Reporting Network (http://www.fcrr.org/pmrn/index.htm)

Research Institute on Progress Monitoring, University of Minnesota (http://www.progressmonitoring.net)

Student-led IEPs

McGahee, M., Mason, C., Wallace, T., & Jones, B. (2001). *Student-led IEPs: A guide for student Involvement.* Arlington, VA: Council for Exceptional Children.

Mason, C.Y., McGahee-Kovac, M., & Johnson, L. (2004). How to help students lead their IEP meetings. *Teaching Exceptional Children, 36*(1), 18–25.

Pacer Center (http://www.pacer.org/tatral/resources/studentiep.asp)

Self-Determination Resource (http://www.selfdeterminationak.org)

Thoma, C., & Wehman, P. (2010). *Getting the most out of IEPs: An educator's guide to the student-directed approach.* Baltimore: Paul H. Brookes Publishing Co.

REFERENCES

Agran, M., & Hughes, C. (2008). Students' opinions regarding their individualized education program involvement. *Career Development for Exceptional Individuals, 31*(2), 69–76.

Ahearn, E. (2006). Standards-based IEPs: Implementation in selected states. *Forum: In Depth Policy Analysis.* Alexandria, VA: Project Forum of the National Association of State Directors of Special Education.

Allen, S.K., Smith, A.C., Test, D.W., Flowers, C. & Wood, W.M. (2001). The effects of self-directed IEP on student participation in their IEP meetings. *Career Development for Exceptional Individuals, 24*(1), 107–120.

Baker, J.M. & Zigmond, N. (1995). The meaning and practice of inclusion for students with learning disabilities: Themes and implications from the five cases. *The Journal of Special Education, 29,* 163–180.

Barrie, W., & McDonald, J. (2002). Administrative support for student-led individualized education programs. *Remedial and Special Education, 23,* 116–122.

Capizzi, A.M. (2008). From assessment to annual goal: Engaging a decision-making process in writing measureable IEPs. *Teaching Exceptional* Children, *41*(1), 18–25.

Cortiella, C. (2008). *Advocacy brief: Understanding the standards-based individualized education program (IEP).* National Center for Learning Disabilities (http://www.LD.org).

Espin, C.A., Deno, S.L., & Albayrak-Kaymak, D. (1998). Individual education programs in resource and inclusive settings: How "individualized" are they? *Journal of Special Education, 32*(2), 164–174.

Etscheidt, S.K. (2006). Progress monitoring: Legal issues and recommendations for IEP teams. *Teaching Exceptional Children, 38*(3), 56–60.

Hammer, M.R. (2004). Using the self-advocacy strategy to increase student participation in IEP conferences. *Intervention in School and Clinic, 39*(5), 295–300.

Holbrook, M.D. (2007). *A seven-step process to creating standards-based IEPs.* Project FORUM, National Association of State Directors of Special Education (http://www.projectforum.org).

Illinois State Board of Education. (1997). *Illinois learning standards.* Available online at http://www.isbe.state.il.us/ILS/

Individuals with Disabilities Education Act Amendments of 1997, PL 105-17, 20 U.S.C. §§ 1400 *et seq.*

Individuals with Disabilities Education Improvement Act of 2004, PL 108-446, 20 U.S.C. §§ 1400 *et seq.*

Konrad, M. (2008). Twenty ways to involve students in the IEP process. *Intervention in School and Clinic, 43*(4), 236–239.

Lee-Tarver, C.A. (2006). Are individualized education plans a good thing? A survey of teachers' perceptions of the utility of IEPs in the regular education setting. *Journal of Instructional Psychology, 33*(4), 263–271.

Lynch, S., & Adams, P. (2008). Developing standards-based individualized education program objectives for students with significant needs. *Teaching Exceptional Children, 40*(3), 36–39.

Martin, J.E., & Marshall, L.H. (1995). Choicemaker: A comprehensive self-determination transition program. *Intervention in School and Clinic, 30,* 147–156.

Martin, J.E., Marshall, L.H., Maxson, L.M., & Jerman, P.L. (1997). *The self-directed IEP.* Longmont, CO: Sopris West.

Martin, J.E., Marshall, L.H., & Sale, R.P. (2004). A 3-year study of middle, junior high, and high school meetings. *Exceptional Children, 70*(3), 285–297.

Martin, J.E., Van Dycke, J.L., Christensen, W.R., Greene, B.A., Gardner, J.E., & Lovett, D.L. (2006). Increasing student participation in IEP meetings: Establishing the self-directed IEP as an evidence-based practice. *Exceptional Children, 72*(3), 299–316.

Mason, C.Y., McGahee-Kovac, M., & Johnson, L. (2004). How to help students lead their IEP meetings. *Teaching Exceptional Children, 36*(1), 18–25.

Mason, C.Y., McGahee-Kovac, M., Johnson, L., & Stillerman, S. (2002). Implementing student-led IEPs: Student participation and student and teacher reactions. *Career Development of Exceptional Individuals, 25,* 171–192.

McGahee, M., Mason, C., Wallace, T., & Jones, B. (2001). *Student-led IEPs: A guide for student Involvement.* Arlington, VA: Council for Exceptional Children.

Nolet, V., & McLaughlin, M.J. (2005). *Accessing the general curriculum: Including students with disabilities in standards-based reform* (2nd ed.). Thousand Oaks, CA: Corwin.

Project FORUM, National Association for State Directors of Special Education (NASDSE) (1998). *Involvement of general education teachers in the IEP process.* Quick Turn Around Forum. Alexandria, VA: Author.

Project FORUM, National Association for State Directors of Special Education (NASDSE) (1999). *Linkage of the IEP to the general education curriculum.* Quick Turn Around Forum. Alexandria, VA: Author.

Snyder, E.P. (2002). Teaching students with combined behavioral disorders and mental retardation to lead their own IEP meetings. *Behavioral Disorders, 27,* 340–357.

Snyder, E.P., & Shapiro, E. (1997). Teaching students with emotional disorders the skills to participate in the development of their IEPs. *Behavioral Disorders, 22,* 246–259.

Thurlow, M.L. (2002). Positive educational results: The promise of standards-based reform. *Remedial and Special Education, 23*(4), 195–202.

VanReusen, A.K., Deshler, D.D., & Shumaker, J.B. (1984). Effects of a student participation strategy in facilitating the involvement of adolescents with learning disabilities in the individualized educational program planning process. *Learning Disabilities, 1*(2), 23–34.

Wehmeyer, M.L., & Palmer, S.B. (2003). Adult outcomes for students with cognitive disabilities three years out of high school: The impact of self-determination. *Education and Training in Developmental Disabilities, 38,* 131–144.

Wehmeyer, M.L., & Schwartz, M. (1997). Self-determination and positive adult outcomes: A follow-up study of youth with mental retardation or learning disabilities. *Exceptional Children, 63*(2), 245–255.

Zigmond, N., & Baker, J.M. (1995). Concluding comments: Current and future practices in inclusive schooling. *Journal of Special Education, 29*(2), 245–250.

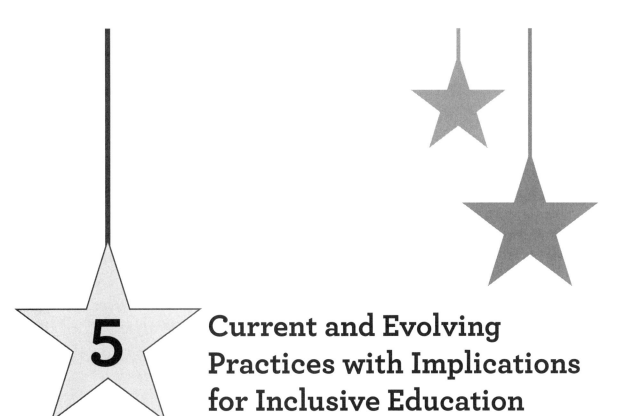

5 Current and Evolving Practices with Implications for Inclusive Education

This chapter focuses on the characteristics and implications of three evolving areas of practice:

1. Maximizing access to the general curriculum

2. Incorporating universal design for learning (UDL) into classroom materials and instruction

3. Implementing response-to-intervention (RTI) models that involve progress monitoring and graduated levels of instructional intensity

These three areas of practice are often merged or intertwined in the professional literature as aspects of an overarching approach to increasing success of all learners in the general education curriculum/setting and as means to establishing accountability for both teachers and learners.

Although the discourse on these areas of practice has not focused on their effect on inclusiveness, such a potential clearly exists. School leaders must be aware of how initiatives may promote or undermine their existing commitment to maximize inclusiveness. Thoughtful leadership is needed to translate concepts and models into everyday practices that are consistent with the overall mission of inclusive education.

MAXIMIZING ACCESS TO THE GENERAL CURRICULUM

The term *access to the general curriculum* gained prominence in the fields of special and inclusive education as a result of language used in the 1997 and 2004 reauthorizations of the IDEA, which specified that students with disabilities should be provided access to the general curriculum. Intensifying the focus on access was consistent with a broader initiative to increase expectations for all students, including those with special needs, and reflected concerns that the use of specialized or individualized curricula may lead to a widening of the achievement gap, as indicated in failing test scores.

Nolet and McLaughlin (2005, p. 3) highlighted the following requirements for IEPs that speak directly to access to the general curriculum and service in the general education classroom:

- A statement of the child's present levels of academic achievement and functional performance, including how the disability affects the child's involvement and progress in the general curriculum
- For children who take alternate assessments aligned to alternative achievement standards, a description of benchmarks or short-term objectives
- Measurable annual goals, including academic and functional goals designed to enable the child to be involved in and progress in the general education curriculum, while also meeting the child's unique needs
- An explanation of the extent, if any, to which the child will not participate with the children without disabilities in the general education class and activities

Increased focus on the general curriculum represents a shift in emphasis from making progress toward both individualized goals and the academic curriculum to achieving on the same curriculum as same-age peers without disabilities. Explicit linkage to the general education curriculum dovetails with provisions of NCLB requiring learning standards and implementation of accountability measures, as well as reflected perceptions that a focus on access to the general curriculum would result in higher expectations and hence achievement (Hardman & Dawson, 2008). In addition, increased focus on the general curriculum is a departure from earlier thinking that a special curriculum is more appropriate for students with disabilities, and that "retrofitting" it to allow access is best achieved through accommodations and modifications implemented by the special educator (Hitchcock, Meyer, Rose, & Jackson, 2002).

Various definitions of *access* and *curriculum* have been discussed in the literature. School leaders who are attempting to use access as a philosophy or framework must begin by establishing a shared understanding. Table 5.1 describes three progressive levels of access and the necessary conditions for ensuring all are met. Many schools have made gains in the first two levels and have started to look closely at maximizing progress, partly because of the adequate yearly progress requirements of NCLB. Inclusive efforts that focus primarily on the physical placement of students with disabilities in general education classrooms may risk the second part of the equation for inclusive education: placement *plus* program.

The term *curriculum* has many different meanings. Leadership is needed to establish a shared understanding by all stakeholders. The general curriculum might be defined as the academic curriculum, as often represented by learning standards and indicators, or as the "full range of experiences students have in school" (Browder, Wakeman, & Flowers, 2006, p. 250). The more narrow interpretation focused on the academic curriculum is useful when the goals are to increase academic achievement, link IEP goals more closely to academic achievement, and improve performance on high-stakes assessments. However, the broader perspective of the curriculum as the composite of experiences in the lives of typical students is more consistent with the goals of inclusive education that include and exceed academic achievement.

Leadership is required for schools to achieve all three levels of access in Table 5.1. Achievement requires the coordinated efforts of administrators, general educators, special educators, specialists, and paraprofessionals. King-Sears (2001, pp. 68–74) described a three-

Table 5.1. Elements and conditions of access to the general curriculum

	Level 1: Exposure	Level 2: Engagement	Level 3: Progress
What happens	The general education curriculum is aligned with learning standards. Instruction for all students is anchored in the general curriculum.	The methods and materials used to deliver the general curriculum are designed to maximize understanding by all learners, including those with special needs.	Student learning is maximized through progress monitoring and adjustments in instruction and supports as needed to facilitate progress.
What it takes	• A clearly defined curriculum with grade-level expectations • Alignment of curriculum with relevant learning standards • Expectation that all staff will implement the general curriculum on a consistent basis for all learners	• Curriculum methods and materials designed for classroom of learners with diverse abilities • Implementation of curricular and instructional modifications designed to meet unique needs of learners with special needs • Individualized education programs for students with special needs target improved performance on the general curriculum.	• Design and implementation of assessments that reflect progress on the curriculum • Use of progress monitoring data to make adjustments to whole-class instruction or supports for individual students

step process for facilitating access by learners with disabilities. The major steps and examples of related activities are as follows:

1. *Analyze the general curriculum:* Activities include evaluating clarity of learning goals, identifying resources, and pinpointing universal design elements presently available

2. *Enhance areas of the general education curriculum that are poorly designed:* Major activity involves enhancing the existing curriculum by building in strategies such as expanding background knowledge, adding examples, incorporating judicious review, or providing visual organizers

3. *Consider creative ways students with disabilities can access the curriculum, including minor to major modifications of outcomes:* Strategies include implementing accommodations (e.g., audio recordings of text), modifying/adapting expectations (e.g., reduced number of pages and required elements in an essay), or introducing parallel curriculum outcomes

   Kluth, Biklen, and Straut (2003) asserted that providing access to academics for all learners may require us to adopt new perceptions of learners (and learning), in addition to using specific instructional practices. These authors cited the following classroom practices for encouraging success in the general education curriculum:

1. Appreciate and teach to learning differences (e.g., differentiate and account for learning styles)

2. Consider lesson authenticity and relevance (e.g., engage students in real-world problem solving)

3. Share "what works" (e.g., teachers share personal knowledge of individual student's strengths and how they learn best)

4. Encourage voice and dialogue (e.g., arrange opportunities for students to be active participants in dialogue about their learning)

5. Value and build on the literacies that students bring to the classroom (e.g., use an "expanded vision" of literacy that includes conversation and discussion, performances such as storytelling, and listening)

Together, the recommended strategies for maximizing access emphasize our perceptions of students as unique and capable. They can be used as a framework for designing curriculum and instruction that is anchored in the expectations of the general education curriculum.

Clearly, maximizing access is best approached as a schoolwide philosophy, guideline, or framework that serves to inform decisions regarding curricula, scheduling, allocation of staff and resources, and composition of class rosters. Maximizing access cannot be achieved with a single intervention or program, but rather through a thoughtfully organized framework for organizing resources, delivering supports, and solving problems.

For middle and high school teachers, teaching content to a diverse group of learners is particularly challenging in that it requires both content knowledge and a repertoire of instructional skills and strategies. Based on their research on inclusive middle/secondary classrooms, Lenz and Deshler (2004, p. 11) have developed the following six goals for inclusive teaching:

1. Be smarter about curriculum and curriculum planning

2. Develop an inclusive learning community

3. Create classroom communications systems

4. Enhance critical content

5. Teach learning strategies

6. Work collaboratively and use support personnel effectively

The first goal involves careful planning of instruction during the initial instruction in the general education classroom to ensure maximum access and success for all learners. The SMARTER planning process (Lenz, Bulgren, Kissam, & Taymans, 2004) guides teams in planning units and coordinating supports for inclusive middle and secondary classrooms. Figure 5.1 summarizes the steps in the SMARTER planning process, which emphasizes anticipating differences in the challenge level of specific content and the strengths and challenges of a diverse class of students. De-emphasizing specific roles in favor of a coordinated effort toward designing and delivering content enhancements and supports is implicit in the planning process.

In the Good High Schools project, researchers sought to identify exemplary high schools for students with disabilities (Morocco, Aguilar, Brigham, Clay, & Zigmond, 2006). Box 5.1 summarizes this project and describes the unique and innovative ways in which the schools maximized access through a collection of curricular and instructional policies and supports. Most notable among the characteristics of the schools were the "ensembles" of academic support and an expanded view of access that emphasized both academic and social achievement.

Maximizing access to the general curriculum is increasingly complex for learners with more significant disabilities, including cognitive disabilities, autism, or multiple disabilities. The extent to which such a focus may or may not serve a student's most pressing needs has been discussed in the professional literature (e.g., Agran, Alper, & Wehmeyer, 2002; Hardman

Shape the critical questions
- Transform learning standards, essential learnings, and instructional objectives into a concise set of critical questions that guide instruction and inform students of what is most important for students to learn

Map the critical content
- Construct a content map that provides a graphic representation of the content in a format that helps readers understand connections and relationships between concepts within the unit

Analyze the difficulties
- Consider which elements of the content will be most challenging for the learners in your class, which requires knowledge of your learners' characteristics and identification of the specific demands placed on students throughout the unit

Reach enhancement decisions
- Consider what types of teaching devices (e.g., mnemonic devices) or teaching routines (e.g., use of graphic organizers) can be used to help anticipate and minimize the impact of learner challenges on progress in the general curriculum

Teach strategically
- Encourage students to act strategically upon the content by modeling and communicating the values of strategy use; provide graphic organizers that allow students to see how information fits together

Evaluate mastery
- Reflect on the effectiveness of specific techniques used in the planning process and determine which produced the desired student outcomes

Revisit outcomes
- Determine if students have mastered critical information and whether reteaching is warranted or required

Figure 5.1. Steps and sample tasks in the SMARTER Planning Process. (*Source:* Lenz, Bulgren, Kissam, & Taymans [2004].)

& Dawson, 2008; Lashley, 2002). At issue is the extent to which the general curriculum is relevant to the learners with significant special needs—learners for whom alternative, functional curricula have been recommended. Research on effective practices for improving access to learners with significant disabilities suggests four general approaches: peer support interventions; teaching self-determination skills; implementing UDL; and teaching and assessing content standards (Spooner, Dymond, Smith, & Kennedy, 2006). Access can also be improved by augmenting the general curriculum and providing instruction on specific strategies. Students may be taught to use learning strategies and tools such as graphic organizers and mnemonic devices to support understanding and retrieval of content. Self-determination skills such as goal setting and problem solving enable students to gain independence from their teacher and solicit the support needed to work in the challenging general curriculum (Lee et al., 2006).

Figure 5.2 presents a decision-making flowchart for maximizing access to the general curriculum while also providing instruction on the unique needs of a learner with a cognitive disability. Teams supporting learners with significant needs must consider how best to use

Box 5.1. ★ Maximizing access: The Good High Schools project

The August 2006 issue of *Learning Disabilities Research & Practice* was dedicated to the Good High Schools project, in which researchers sought to identify three high schools where students with learning disabilities were experiencing success in academic achievement, social relationships, and preparation for life after high school (Morocco, Aguilar, Clay, Brigham, & Zigmond, 2006).

To be considered, schools had to be academically excellent in an urban setting, committed to inclusion of students with disabilities in general education classes, and serve a diverse student population. The three finalists included schools in New York, Virginia, and Florida, all of which maximized access to and achievement in the general curriculum through the following structures and strategies:

1. *Academic choice:* Students with learning disabilities enrolled in the general education courses, some with modifications such as an extended duration or a smaller class size. In addition, open enrollment was allowed for advanced courses and students were encouraged to take electives. Students were not "tracked" into lower level or remedial classes.

2. *Ensembles of academic support*: Each school provided a variety of traditional and innovative supports coordinated on a schoolwide level to promote consistency. "Signature practices" included coteaching, focus on big ideas and questions, and strategy instruction.

3. *Encouragement to participate in school activities:* Students were provided with a wide range of cocurricular activities, for which participation was encouraged and supported (not just left to chance). Students were encouraged to establish social networks and to self-advocate for themselves with others.

4. *Strong sense of community among adults:* Teachers and administrators viewed themselves as partners, not as representatives of distinct general education and special education programs. General educators assumed shared responsibility for students with disabilities, and special educators provided input on curricular and instructional decisions.

5. *Responsive leadership:* General education and special education administrators collaborated to promote practices that balanced emphasis on the success of individual students and accountability for the school as a whole. Where tensions arose, such as around budgeting issues, school leaders worked together to preserve the commitment to inclusiveness while maintaining high standards for all students.

specialized services such as occupational therapy, physical therapy, and speech–language therapy to promote access to the general curriculum. Assistive technologies play a more prominent role in providing access for learners with more significant needs, as does more intensive instruction on specific skills, typically delivered in small-group instruction. Thus, teams not only must consider what supports are needed to maximize access, but also how to deliver supports in the general education classroom.

One approach to delivering instruction to individual students is to embed the instruction within the normal routine of the classroom (McDonnell, Johnson, & McQuivey, 2008).

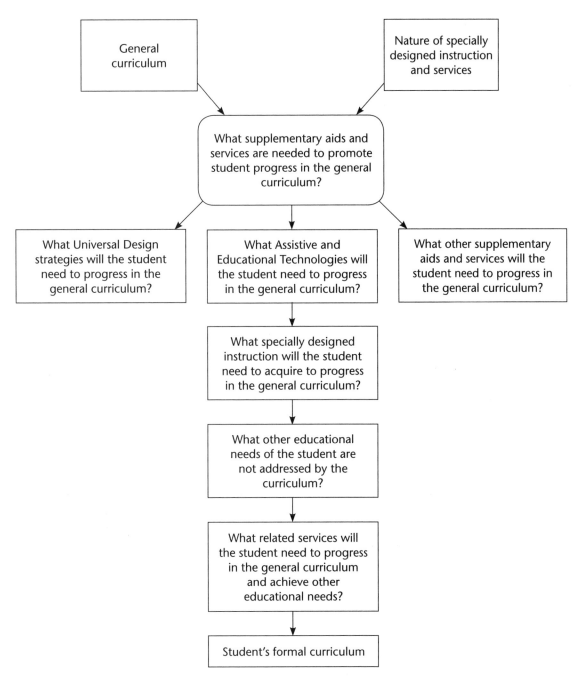

Figure 5.2. Individualized education program team decision-making process to promote student progress in the general education curriculum. (Republished with permission of Routledge, from "Universal Design for Learning, Access to the General Education Curriculum and Students with Mild Mental Retardation" by M.L. Wehmeyer, 2006, *Exceptionality, 14(4)*, p. 232; permission conveyed through Copyright Clearance Center, Inc.)

For example, students may receive additional instruction on vocabulary words during a transition period for the entire classroom or instruction can be interspersed with that for the whole class (Johnson, McDonnell, Holzwarth, & Hunter, 2004).

Grading practices should be included in a discussion of inclusive practices. Letter or number grades students receive are one indicator of progress, and low or failing grades often trigger placement and program considerations for students with special needs. Grading policies that benefit all students emphasize the alignment of the elements (e.g., tests, projects) used to determine a report card grade with the knowledge and skills required in the relevant learning standards for the school. Some schools engage in explicit standards-based grading practices, whereas others take steps to ensure that the elements that "count" for grading are those that are based on the most important content for a given grade level (Guskey, 2001; O'Connor, 2009). A major concern for students with special needs is the increased risk of low or failing grades, particularly in the middle and high school grades. Classwide practices that benefit all learners include not giving zeroes for missing work, as well as using different types of assessments that allow learner choice and provide alternatives when a particular type of assessment (e.g., timed essay tests) "interacts" with a learner's challenges to produce a score that may not accurately reflect what has been learned (Guskey & Bailey, 2001; Wormeli, 2006). In general, teams should seek to minimize zeroes by providing supports (e.g. homework communication systems) that increase work completion and allow students to turn in late work for credit.

Teams must also monitor grades closely and react quickly to a series of low or failing grades by engaging in problem solving. A general problem-solving approach involves pinpointing the types of assignments or expectations that are producing low grades, determining the extent to which the specific assignments interact with the learner's learning challenges, reviewing the current accommodations or modifications, determining the need for improving delivery or adding new supports or motivational strategies, and establishing a plan for monitoring progress on a regular basis (Munk, 2003). An outcome of the problem-solving process might also be a decision to individualize the grading system by changing the grading elements (Munk, 2003) or to establish that the student will be graded on progress toward an alternative learning standard, typically at a lower level (Jung, 2009; Jung & Guskey, 2007). School leaders who develop policy and enforce practices must emphasize the need to communicate to students, parents, and teachers how grades are determined, the importance of using the classwide practices that benefit all learners, and the importance of monitoring their student's grades and initiating problem solving when they are low. The most important message for leaders to send to students, parents, and teams is that grading issues can be addressed within the general education classroom. The needs for problem solving and perhaps an individualized system are not valid reasons to move learners to a special classroom.

Table 5.2 presents the STAR organizer for maximizing access to the general education curriculum.

UNIVERSAL DESIGN FOR LEARNING

The concept of universal design as applied to teaching and learning (often referred to as UDL) embodies a collection of curricular and instructional techniques all designed to make the general curriculum more accessible to learners with diverse abilities. A unique aspect of UDL is that the curriculum and instructional methods are designed to anticipate differences among learners, with the intent of allowing a student in an inclusive classroom to take advantage of design features that fit his or her particular needs, while classmates may be using a different feature or support to meet their own needs.

The foundation for the UDL framework is brain imaging research indicating that three neural networks—recognition, strategic, and affective—are used during learning. The way in which we deliver instruction can make the best (or worst) use of these neural networks (Rose & Meyer, 2002). To anticipate the different ways in which students recognize information and act strategically on what they see or hear, as well as how they feel about what they

STAR ORGANIZER

Table 5.2.

FOR MAXIMIZING ACCESS TO THE GENERAL EDUCATION CURRICULUM

AREA OF PRACTICE	SAMPLE LEADERSHIP ACTIVITIES
Setting the tone	• Establish a shared vision of progress in the general education curriculum as the goal for all students. • Include access to the agenda for all curriculum adoption instructions. • Set the expectation that all teachers are responsible for planning and designing instruction that is designed for a diverse classroom of learners. • Emphasize to staff that students with challenging behaviors are members of the school community who deserve to be taught the skills necessary for positive social interaction.
 **Translating research into practice**	• Follow the general guidelines in Chapter 2 (Table 2.3) for identifying, implementing, and evaluating new practices. • Develop IEPs that focus on skills critical to success in the general curriculum. • Develop IEPs for students with significant needs that balance progress in the general curriculum and functional needs of the individual student. • Arrange for staff to share strategies proven effective for students with academic or behavioral challenges in the general education setting.
 **Arranging for collaboration**	• Provide meeting time for teams to review expectations of the general curriculum and identify areas in which students with special needs will require differentiation, additional support, or accommodations to be successful. • Hold weekly grade-level team meetings for planning and organizing supports. • Inform parents of the expectation of the general curriculum and provide guidance on how they can help their child at home. • Coordinate homework to avoid overload.
 **Reflecting on processes and outcomes**	• Continuously monitor progress on common assessments. • Conduct monthly evaluation of teaming practices to determine if staff time and expertise are being used to balance the need to move forward in the curriculum with individual student needs.

Table 5.3.   Guiding principles of universal design for learning and examples of classroom implementation

Guiding principle	Classroom examples
Provide multiple means of representation (to support diverse recognition networks).	• Students in a science class are encouraged to seek information on how information is transmitted by waves from multiple sources, including the science text, online sources, videos, supplementary texts written for a higher- or lower-grade level, or live presentation from a teacher or qualified adult, such as a radio or television technician.
Provide multiple means of action and expression (to support diverse strategic networks).	• Students are provided options for engaging information on waves and demonstrating their understanding. Options might include creating a report to share with their classmates, providing a demonstration of wave transmittal in class, completing a test prepared by the teacher, creating a graphic display for classmates to view, preparing and teaching a brief lesson on one aspect of wave transmission.
	• Students are provided support from the teacher in ways and at times that meet their needs. Teacher support is scaffolded based on student need. Opportunities for formative feedback and practice are readily available.
Provide multiple means of engagement (to support diverse affective networks).	• Students are allowed to choose the level of challenge at which they wish to work. For example, students with background knowledge may choose a more complex project that extends their expertise.
	• Students are provided options about where and when they will complete their work. For example, some students may wish to dissect a radio transmitter outside the classroom.
	• Students help to choose rewards. For example, a student may be involved in creating the evaluation rubric for his or her work and will be allowed to self-evaluate the final product.

are learning, UDL incorporates the three guiding principles described in Table 5.3 (Coyne et al., 2006; Rose & Meyer, 2002).

Perhaps because UDL is generally considered a philosophy or approach represented by a number of specific strategies or tools, research on specific applications of UDL and student achievement are emerging in a variety of sources (Johnstone, 2003; National Center on Universal Design for Learning, 2009). Early applications of UDL have mainly focused on moving beyond the traditional print textbook as a primary source of information. Print materials are an omnipresent barrier for learners who struggle with reading decoding and comprehension, who are still learning English, or who have limited vision. Past practices to improve accessibility have included Braille, audiotexts, enlarged print, and electronic text (Stahl, 2006). Technological developments have enhanced access to digital text and IDEA of 2004 included provisions for creation of the National Instructional Materials Accessibility Standard, which requires that "print instructional materials" used by schools must be made available in "specialized formats" that include Braille, audio, or digital text (http://www.idea partnerships.org). The U.S. Department of Education Office of Special Education Programs funds a National Instructional Materials Accessibility Standard Technical Assistance Center, which provides information on how to create materials that conform to standards and resources for approved materials. This information is supported by the Center for Applied Special Technology and is available by contacting their website (http://aim.cast.org). Digital sources such as e-books incorporate features such as online libraries, text-to-speech capability, and options for manipulating font size and color that function as accommodations for struggling readers (Cavanaugh, 2002). Examples of electronic versions of popular texts (e.g.,

The Call of the Wild) with integrated tools and strategies to maximize comprehension are available from the Center for Applied Special Technology (http://www.cast.org/Teaching EveryStudent/ncac).

Perhaps the most important aspect of UDL is that it involves a proactive approach to instructing and assessing diverse groups of learners. It therefore requires collaboration between general and special educators in the design of instruction. Universal design negates or limits the need for "retrofitting" general education instruction and materials to meet the needs of learners with special needs, which is a time-consuming process that often results in learners having to be separated from their classmates (Hitchcock et al., 2002). The Center for Applied Special Technology has designed free, online tools to guide in the design and evaluation of curriculum and lesson plans that incorporate features of UDL. Figure 5.3 presents one of the tools; additional tools are available for developing digital books, accessing electronic texts, and building lessons (http://www.cast.org).

WELCOME!

Welcome to the CAST Universal Design for Learning (UDL) Curriculum Self-Check

Use this site to help you apply UDL principles in your teaching to reach and engage **all** of your students. The goal of UDL is to enable all individuals to gain knowledge, skills and enthusiasm for learning. Learn about UDL, Check Your Curriculum, or Explore Resources for ideas on how to build options and flexibility into each element of your curriculum.

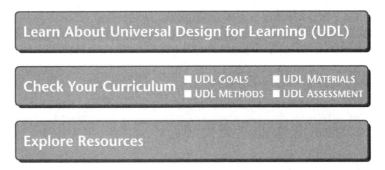

Figure 5.3. Online tool for implementing universal design for learning. (From CAST web site http://udlselfcheck.cast.org/ Copyright © 2010 CAST; reprinted by permission.)

Preservice general and special teachers who have experience with UDL in their preparation programs are better prepared to integrate critical features into their original lesson plans for an inclusive classroom (VanLaarhoven, Munk, Lynch, Bosma, & Rouse, 2007; VanLaarhoven et al., 2006). Teachers of preparation programs must be cognizant of their role in preparing new teachers to use UDL as a framework for designing curriculum and instruction (Jiminez, Graf, & Rose, 2007). Clearly, proficiency with technologies (e.g., hardware, software, external devices) that minimize the impact of learning or language differences on the "inputs" for information and the "outputs" students generate should be a priority for enhancing inclusive practices. Assistive technologies for learners can be recommended by a learner's IEP team. However, research suggests that use varies among schools and teams; in many cases, the classroom teachers are not adequately prepared to support their students in using technology effectively (Smith & Allsopp, 2005), or it is underutilized for students with milder disabilities. For technology to be utilized efficiently toward UDL, practices in general education instructional technology and those in assistive technology must be merged (Edyburn, 2004). For this to happen, school leaders must establish structures in which specialists in instructional and assistive technologies work in concert, with shared responsibility for the entire student body. Table 5.4 presents the STAR organizer for implementing universal design for learning.

RESPONSE TO INTERVENTION

IDEA of 2004 included provisions and incentives for states to adopt RTI models for identifying students with learning disabilities. RTI represents an alternative to the traditional IQ achievement discrepancy model that typically compares performance on standardized tests, including those for intelligence, and actual classroom achievement. Students with "average" or above intelligence who scored lower on measures of academic achievement and on actual classroom work could be diagnosed with a learning disability. In contrast, the RTI model relies on evidence of a student's performance on high-quality, scientifically based instruction. Ongoing assessment data are used to make instructional decisions and to identify students who need supplemental or intensive instruction to achieve at a satisfactory level. Hence, the term *instruction* is sometimes substituted for *intervention* in RTI.

The most common conceptualization of an RTI model involves a series of tiered interventions that progress from least to most intensive and that involve regular progress monitoring as criteria for placement of students into the most appropriate tier. Figure 5.4 presents a visual depiction of the three tiers of intervention for both academic and social-emotional skills. Research on the prevalence of academic and behavioral problems among students provides for estimates of the number of students who will require the more intensive services in Tiers 2 and 3 (Batsche et al., 2006).

Although RTI has been promoted and tested as a model for identifying learning disabilities (Vaughn, Linan-Thompson, & Hickman, 2003), it can also provide a useful framework for supporting students in an inclusive setting. Table 5.5 presents a general model for RTI that incorporates features recommended in the professional literature (e.g., Bender & Shores, 2007; Fuchs & Fuchs, 2001; Wright, 2007), which is currently used in schools familiar to these authors. In ensuring high-quality instruction for all students in Tier 1 and responding quickly to slow progress with supplemental, intensive support (Tier 2), teams maximize access to the general curriculum and implement small-group instruction that is based on performance, not disability. Figure 5.5 presents a research-tested, multitiered model for reading

STAR ORGANIZER

FOR IMPLEMENTING
UNIVERSAL DESIGN FOR LEARNING

Table 5.4.

AREA OF PRACTICE	SAMPLE LEADERSHIP ACTIVITIES
Setting the tone	· Model universal design for learning (UDL) by providing information to staff and parents in a variety of formats. · Recruit staff who are familiar with the principles of UDL and open to implementing emerging technologies. · Establish a unified vision for technology use that merges instructional technology with assistive technology.
 **Translating research into practice**	· Follow the general guidelines in Chapter 2 (Table 2.3) for identifying, implementing, and evaluating new practices. · Provide professional development on how to incorporate UDL in the design of curricular materials and instructional methods. · Design a web site for sharing examples of effective UDL strategies. · Establish supportive learning communities focused on gaining expertise in use of technology to differentiate instruction and assessment. · Prioritize purchase of equipment, tools, or software that has a research base and can be used in the general education setting.
 **Arranging for collaboration**	· Spotlight effective use of UDL at team and faculty meetings. · Inform parents of principles of UDL and how it will be implemented in your school. · Build in time for team planning to identify electronic sources for content and how technology can be provided to improve student access and allow for valid assessment. · Provide professional development so that all team members are familiar with assistive technologies and are prepared to determine the appropriateness of a specific device or tool for an individual student.
 **Reflecting on processes and outcomes**	· Survey staff on familiarity and comfort level with various forms of technology. · Continuously monitor student performance on common assessments in which UDL was incorporated. · Have district technology committee solicit feedback from parents, students, and teachers on which technologies are most helpful.

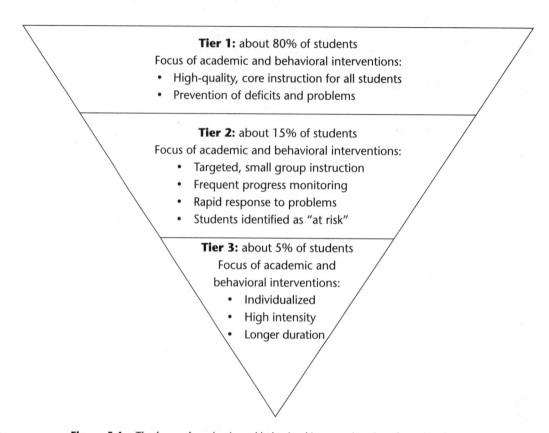

Figure 5.4.   The focus of academic and behavioral interventions in a three-tiered system.

instruction that involves enhancements to the whole class instruction with a basal reading program (Bursuck & Damer, 2011; Bursuck et al., 2004).

As indicated in Figure 5.4, the multitiered approach to assessment and intervention includes social-emotional (prosocial) behaviors and academics. At the Tier 1 level of intervention, programs focusing on prevention of and rapid response to problem behaviors have garnered attention. Positive behavior intervention and supports (http://www.pbis.org) have emerged as one model for behavior interventions that can be constructed as a multitiered model consistent with the goals of RTI. Increased emphasis on schoolwide programs that are proactive and preventative has supplanted more traditional discipline systems that rely primarily on the response to problem behaviors. In addition, programs focused on prevention emphasize implementation by all staff, with shared responsibility for all students, including those with special needs. The role of the general education staff is elevated in a schoolwide, preventative program.

Implementing a Tier 1 program with quality and integrity requires substantial leadership on the part of school leaders and teams charged with specific responsibilities related to implementation. Colvin (2007) described a process for developing a proactive discipline plan in a school that includes the following steps:

1. Develop a purpose statement for the schoolwide plan

2. Establish schoolwide behavior expectations

3. Implement strategies to teach behavior expectations to student body

Table 5.5. Steps in the response-to-intervention model for identifying learning disabilities and implications for inclusive education

Model	Practices
Step 1: Universal screening	• Brief assessments are administered to all students in target skill areas (typically three times a year).
	• Teams establish grade-level benchmarks on these key skill areas.
	• Teams review data following each benchmark assessment to determine students at risk of not meeting targets.
	• Academic and behavioral data are reviewed.
Step 2: Implementing classroom instruction (Tier 1)	• Curriculum in all subjects is aligned to standards.
	• Core instruction is research based.
	• Students with special needs are provided with individualized accommodations/modifications.
Step 3: Monitoring responsiveness to Tier 1 classroom instruction	• Common assessments are used to determine student response to instruction.
	• Grade level and/or subject area teams meet to analyze assessment data on a regular basis.
	• Adjustments are made to instruction based on the results of assessment data.
	• Teams analyze multiple sources of information (including universal screening data) to identify students needing supplemental instruction.
Step 4: Implementing supplemental, diagnostic, or specialized instruction (Tier 2)	• A formal problem-solving process is designed for instructional decisions.
	• Students are grouped for instruction based on the specific skills needed for success.
	• Tier 2 instruction uses research-validated methods.
	• Supplemental instruction is provided in addition to and in support of core instruction.
Step 5: Monitoring responsiveness to Tier 2 instruction	• Teachers monitor the progress of Tier 2 students at least two times per month.
	• Progress data is charted and compared to Tier 1 success benchmarks.
	• Ongoing assessment information and performance at Tier 1 are used to determine when supplemental instruction is no longer needed, or whether Tier 3 intensity may be warranted.
Step 6: Comprehensive evaluation of nonresponders to Tier 3 to determine eligibility for special education For all students in need of Tier 3 instruction, decisions are made how to structure day to provide individualized instruction while maximizing access to general education.	• When response to Tier 2 instruction is unsatisfactory, students are referred to the individual problem-solving team (or Tier 3 team).
	• The Tier 3 team reviews data from multiple sources over time to determine if Tier 3 instruction is required.
	• Evidence-based individualized instruction is provided.
	• Teachers monitor progress at least weekly and data are charted to determine if trends will be sufficient to meet established goals.
	• Instruction is changed or adjusted based on response data.
	• If results show that the student needs long term intensive intervention, RTI data, in addition to other performance data, may be used to determine entitlement for special education services.

4. Implement strategies to maintain positive behaviors

5. Implement consequences for negative behaviors

6. Collect and analyze data on the program's impact

7. Develop a plan to sustain the program into the future

Colvin (2007) also recommended that the principal assume the primary role and that a building leadership team be formed to carry out the many responsibilities in implementing

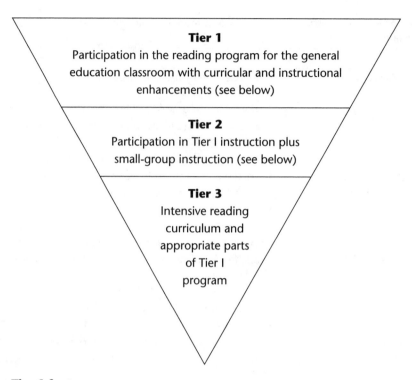

Tier 1 features:

Enhancements: advance organizers, unison responding, efficient use of teacher talk, perky pace, model-lead-test format, cumulative review, systematic error correction, teaching to success, student motivation system

Tier 2 features:

Tier 1 instruction plus additional small-group instruction (three to six students) for 30–40 minutes daily (10 min. for kindergarten)

Tier 3 features:

More intensive reading program delivered in small groups (one to four students) for 60–90 minutes per day

Figure 5.5. Example of a multitiered model for reading instruction. (*Source:* Bursuck & Damer, 2011.)

a schoolwide program. Figure 5.6 depicts a tiered model of behavioral interventions; Table 5.6 presents the STAR Organizer for implementing a response-to-intervention model in your school.

WRAPPING UP AND LOOKING AHEAD

This chapter described three evolving practices in general and special education and highlighted their potential impact on efforts toward inclusive education. Although maximizing access to the general curriculum and RTI share the goal of preventing academic and behavioral problems for all students, their foci are on student achievement in the general curriculum; they may lead to serving students outside of the general education classroom for the purpose of providing more intensive (e.g., Tier 2 or 3) instruction. Thus, it is critical that school leaders highlight the intricate relationship of an inclusive mission to new or evolving

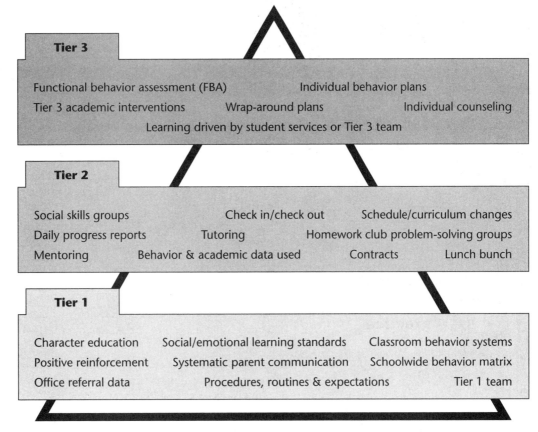

Figure 5.6. Example of multitiered intervention for behavior. (*Source:* Illinois PBIS Network [2008].)

initiatives so that consideration of inclusive education as *placement plus program* is not unintentionally overlooked. For inclusive practices to be sustained, they must be regarded as part of the larger context into which we create new structures, programs, or services. Otherwise, inclusive education, like many other initiatives, will itself be replaced or crowded out by competing goals and ideas.

RECOMMENDED RESOURCES

Access to the General Curriculum

American Institutes for Research ACCESS Center (http://www.k8accesscenter.org)

Beach Center on Disability (http://www.beachcenter.org)

Center on Innovation and Improvement (http://www.centerii.org)

Center for Research and Learning at the University of Kansas (http://www.ku-crl.org)

Kluth, P., Straut, D.M., & Biklen, D.P. (2003). *Access to academics for all students: Critical approaches to inclusive curriculum, instruction, and policy.* Mahwah, NJ: Lawrence Erlbaum Associates.

Learning Disabilities Research & Practice (Vol. 21, August 2006; five articles describing the Good High Schools project)

Lenz, B.K., Deshler, D.D., & Kissam, B.R. (2004). *Teaching content to all: Evidence-based inclusive practices in middle and secondary schools.* Boston: Pearson.

STAR ORGANIZER

FOR IMPLEMENTING
RESPONSE TO INTERVENTION (RTI)

Table 5.6.

AREA OF PRACTICE	SAMPLE LEADERSHIP ACTIVITIES
 **Setting the tone**	• Start the year by presenting a "gap analysis" of data to show performance of school subgroups relative to learning standards over time. • Reinforce the perspective that the goal of RTI is to improve success for all students, and not simply a special education initiative. • Ask the guiding question, "What will it take to maximize the number of students achieving learning standards?"
 **Translating research into practice**	• Follow the general guidelines in Chapter 2 (Table 2.3) for identifying, implementing, and evaluating new practices. • Implement research-validated instructional methods at each tier, based on student needs that emerge from universal screening data. • Organize professional learning by having teams study and share teaching strategies based on principles of universal design (Tier 1 or school improvement team).

 **Arranging for collaboration**	• Establish Tier 1, 2, and 3 teams that analyze ongoing assessment data to formulate instructional practices that successfully result in progress for all students on learning standards.
	  o Tier 1: School improvement team
	  o Tier 2: Grade level/departments
	  o Tier 3: Individual problem solving
	• Develop a protocol for teams to ensure that teams are analyzing progress-monitoring data using a standard problem-solving process.
	• Establish decision rules for teams to identify students who need different instructional strategies and/or change to a different tier of intensity.

 **Reflecting on processes and outcomes**	• Design professional development activities at the team level using the established problem-solving process (e.g., specific strategies for differentiating instruction based on learner needs). • Implement fidelity checks at all instructional tiers to ensure that instruction is consistent with validated research. • Involve teams in data collection and analysis. • The school improvement team analyzes progress-monitoring data from each tier to determine professional development needs.

Nolet, V., & McLaughlin, M.J. (2005). *Accessing the general curriculum: Including students with disabilities in standards-based reform* (2nd ed.). Thousand Oaks, CA: Corwin.

Universal Design for Learning

American Institutes for Research ACCESS Center (http://www.k8accesscenter.org)

Center for Applied Special Technology (http://www.cast.org)

Center for Universal Design at North Carolina State University (http://www.design.ncsu.edu)

IRIS Center for Training Enhancements (http://www.iris.peabody.vanderbilt.edu)

National Center for Accessible Media (http://www.ncam.wgbh.org)

Rose, D.H., & Meyer, A. (2002). *Teaching every student in the digital age: Universal design for learning.* Alexandria, VA: Association for Supervision and Curriculum Development.

Rose, D.H., & Meyer, A.M. (Eds.). (2006). *A practical reader in universal design for learning.* Cambridge, MA: Harvard Education Press.

U.S. Department of Education Office of Special Education Programs (http://www2.ed.gov/about/offices/list/osers/osep/index.html?src=mr)

Universal Design Education (http://www.udeducation.org)

Response to Intervention

Bender, W., & Shores, C. (2007). *Response to intervention: A practical guide for every teacher.* Thousand Oaks, CA: Corwin.

Colvin, G. (2007). *7 steps for developing a proactive schoolwide discipline plan: A guide for principals and leadership teams.* Thousand Oaks, CA: Corwin.

National Association of State Directors of Special Education, IDEA Partnership (http://www.ideapartnership.org/)

National Center on Response to Intervention (http://www.rti4success.org/)

U.S. Department of Education Institute for Education Sciences (http://www.ies.ed.gov/ncee/wwc/publications/practiceguides/)

U.S. Department of Education Office of Special Education Programs Technical Assistance Center on Positive Behavior Interventions and Supports (http://www.PBIS.org)

Wright, J. (2007). *RTI toolkit: A practical guide for schools.* Port Chester, NY: Dude Publishing.

REFERENCES

Agran, M., Alper, S., & Wehmeyer, M. (2002). Access to the general curriculum for students with significant disabilities: What it means to teachers. *Education and Training in Mental Retardation and Developmental Disabilities, 37,* 123–133.

Batsche, G., Elliott, J., Graden, J.L., Grimes, J., Kovaleski, J.F., Prasse, D., et al. (2006). *Response to intervention: Policy considerations and implementation* (4th ed.). Alexandria, VA: National Association of State Directors of Special Education.

Bender, W., & Shores, C. (2007). *Response to intervention: A practical guide for every teacher.* Thousand Oaks, CA: Corwin.

Browder, D.M., Wakeman, S.Y., & Flowers, C. (2006). Assessment of progress in the general curriculum for students with disabilities. *Theory into Practice, 45*(3), 249–259.

Bursuck, W.D., & Damer, M. (2011). *Teaching reading to students who are at risk or have disabilities: A multitier approach* (2nd ed.). Boston: Pearson.

Bursuck, W.D., Smith, T., Munk, D., Damer, M., Mehlig, L., & Perry, J. (2004). Evaluating the impact of a prevention-based model of reading on children at risk. *Remedial and Special Education, 25,* 303–313.

Cavanaugh, T. (2002). EBooks and accommodations: Is this the future of print accommodation? *Teaching Exceptional Children, 35*(2), 56–61.

Colvin, G. (2007). *7 steps for developing a proactive schoolwide discipline plan: A guide for principals and leadership teams.* Thousand Oaks, CA: Corwin.

Coyne, P., Ganley, P., Hall, T., Meo, G., Murray, E., & Gordon, D. (2006). Applying universal design for learning in the classroom. In D.H. Rose & A. Meyer (Eds.), *A practical reader in universal design for learning.* Cambridge, MA: Harvard University Press.

Edyburn, D.L. (2004). Redefining assistive technology. *Special Education Technology Practice, 5*(4), 16–23.

Fuchs, D., & Fuchs, L.S. (2001). Responsiveness-to-intervention: A blueprint for practitioners, policymakers, and parents. *Teaching Exceptional Children, 38*(1), 57–61.

Guskey, T.R. (2001). Helping standards make the grade. *Educational Leadership, 59*(1), 20–27.

Guskey, T.R. (2004). The communication challenge of standards-based reporting. *Phi Delta Kappan, 86,* 326–329.

Guskey, T.R., & Bailey, J.M. (2001). *Developing grading and reporting systems for student learning.* Thousand Oaks, CA: Corwin.

Hardman, M.L. & Dawson, S. (2008). The impact of federal public policy on curriculum and instruction for students with disabilities in the general classroom. *Preventing School Failure, 52, 2,* 5–11.

Hitchcock, C., Meyer, A., Rose, D., & Jackson, R. (2002). Providing access to the general curriculum: Universal design for learning. *Teaching Exceptional Children, 35*(2), 8–17.

Jiminez, T.C., Graf, V.L., & Rose, E. (2007). Gaining access to general education: The promise of universal design for learning. *Issues in Teacher Education, 16*(2), 41–54.

Johnson, J.W., McDonnell, J., Holzwarth, V., & Hunter, K. (2004). The efficacy of embedded instruction for students with developmental disabilities enrolled in general education classes. *Journal of Positive Behavioral Interventions, 6,* 214–227.

Johnstone, C.J. (2003). *Improving validity of large-scale tests: Universal design and student performance* (Technical Report 37). Minneapolis, MN: University of Minnesota, National Center on Educational Outcomes. Retrieved November 29, 2009, from http://education.umn.edu/NCEO/OnlinePubs/Technical37.htm.

Jung, L.A. (2009). The challenges of grading and reporting in special education: An inclusive grading model. In T.R. Guskey (Ed.), *Practical solutions for serious problems in standards-based grading.* Thousand Oaks, CA: Corwin.

Jung, L.A., & Guskey, T.R. (2007). Standards-based grading and reporting: A model for special education. *Teaching Exceptional Children, 40*(2), 48–53.

King-Sears, M.E. (2001). Three steps for gaining access to the general education curriculum for learners with disabilities. *Intervention in School and Clinic, 37*(2), 67–76.

Kluth, P., Biklen, D.P., & Straut, D.M. (2003). Access to academics for all students. In P. Kluth, D.M. Straut, & D.P. Biklen (Eds.), *Access to academics for all students: Critical approaches to inclusive curriculum, instruction, and policy.* New York: Routledge.

Lashley, C. (2002). Participation of students with disabilities in statewide assessments and the general education curriculum: Implications for administrative practice. *Journal of Special Education Leadership, 15,* 10–16.

Lee, S.K., Amos, B.A., Gragoudas, S., Lee, Y., Shogren, K.A., Theoharis, R., et al. (2006). Curriculum augmentation and adaptation strategies to promote access to the general curriculum for students with intellectual and developmental disabilities. *Education and Training in Developmental Disabilities, 41*(3), 199–212.

Lenz, B.K., Bulgren, J.A., Kissam, B.R., & Taymans, J. (2004). SMARTER planning for academic diversity. In B.K. Lenz, D.D. Deshler, & B.R. Kissam (Eds.), *Teaching content to all: Evidence-based practices in middle and secondary schools.* Boston: Pearson.

Lenz, B.K., & Deshler, D.D. (2004). Teaching and academic diversity. In B.K. Lenz, D.D. Deshler, & B.R. Kissam (Eds.), *Teaching content to all: Evidence-based practices in middle and secondary schools.* Boston: Pearson.

McDonnell, J., Johnson, J.W., & McQuivey, C. (2008). *Embedded instruction for students with developmental disabilities in general education classrooms.* Arlington, VA: Council for Exceptional Children.

Morocco, C.C., Aguilar, C.M., Clay, K., Brigham, N., & Zigmond, N. (2006). Good high schools for students with disabilities: Introduction to special issue. *Learning Disabilities Research & Practice, 21*(3), 135–145.

Munk, D.D. (2003). *Solving the grading puzzle for students with disabilities.* Whitefish Bay, WI: Knowledge by Design.

National Center on Universal Design for Learning. (2009). *Research to Support UDL Guidelines.* Retrieved March 9, 2009, from http://www.udlcenter.org/aboutudl/udlguidelines/research.

Nolet, V., & McLaughlin, M.J. (2005). *Accessing the general curriculum: Including students with disabilities in standards-based reform* (2nd ed.). Thousand Oaks, CA: Corwin.

O'Connor, K. (2009). *How to grade for learning: K-12.* Thousand Oaks, CA: Corwin.

Rose, D.H., & Meyer, A. (2002). *Teaching every student in the digital age: Universal design for learning.* Alexandria, VA: Association for Supervision and Curriculum Development.

Smith, S.J., & Allsopp, D. (2005). Technology and inservice professional development: Integrating an effective medium to bridge research to practice. In D. Edyburn, K. Higgins, & R. Boone (Eds.), *Handbook of special education technology research and practice.* Whitefish Bay, WI: Knowledge by Design.

Spooner, F., Dymond, S.K., Smith, A., & Kennedy, C.H. (2006). What we know and need to know about accessing the general curriculum for students with significant cognitive disabilities. *Research & Practice for Persons with Severe Disabilities, 31*(4), 277–283.

Stahl, S. (2006). Transforming the textbook to improve learning. In D.H. Rose & A. Meyer (Eds.), *A practical reader in universal design for learning.* Cambridge, MA: Harvard University Press.

VanLaarhoven, T., Munk, D.D., Lynch, K., Bosma, J., & Rouse, J. (2007). Model for preparing special education pre-service teachers for inclusive education. *Journal of Teacher Education, 58,* 440–455.

VanLaarhoven, T., Munk, D.D., Lynch, K., Wyland, S., Dorsch, N., Bosma, J., et al. (2006). Project ACCEPT: Preparing pre-service special and general educators for inclusive education. *Teacher Education and Special Education, 29*(4), 209–212.

Vaughn, S., Linan-Thompson, S., & Hickman, P. (2003). Response to instruction as a means of identifying students with reading/learning disabilities. *Exceptional Children, 69*(4), 391–409.

Wehmeyer, M.L. (2006). Universal design for learning, access to the general education curriculum and students with mild mental retardation. *Exceptionality, 14,* 225–235.

Wormeli, R. (2006). *Fair isn't always equal: Assessing & grading in the differentiated classroom.* Portland, ME: Stenhouse Publishers.

Wright, J. (2007). *RTI toolkit: A practical guide for schools.* Port Chester, NY: Dude Publishing.

Implementing STAR Organizer Activities

Tools to Expedite Your Work

In this book, we present a broad range of topics, issues, trends, and practices that have direct and indirect implications for the inclusiveness of your school. The ultimate goal for each chapter is to provide enough information so that readers can understand the importance of specific topics and thereby be motivated to seek more information from the sources cited or recommended. We reiterate throughout the book that, in effect, inclusive education is never completed in the sense that a product is finished or a defined goal is met. There are simply too many facets and too many potential outcomes for us to ever consider that we have fully achieved inclusiveness and can therefore shift our attention to other initiatives. As stated previously, research suggests that inclusive efforts are difficult to sustain. They are often shoved aside by new initiatives or reallocation of resources, both human and material. Inclusiveness requires vigilance, which in turn requires persistent monitoring and problem solving.

In this chapter, we revisit several topics discussed in Chapters 1–5 and provide examples of tools designed to expedite their implementation. The tools are provided in ready-to-copy format; they also can be used as a model that you can adapt to meet your specific needs. For each tool, we provide a rationale that links to previous chapters; for most tools, we also include suggestions for implementation.

CREATING A SNAPSHOT OF INCLUSION AT YOUR SCHOOL OR DISTRICT (TOOL 6.1)

The percentage of time that students spend in the general education setting in the United States is depicted in Table 1.1; the extent to which those percentages have changed over time is evidenced in Table 1.2. Such data provide the placement component of the *placement plus program* formula that we recommend for inclusive education. Therefore, it is a logical place to establish a baseline of inclusiveness in your district. The quality of the program component of the formula may be evidenced in outcome data, such as performance of students with special

Time spent in general education classrooms

Level of special need	80% or more of day	79%–40% of day	Less than 40% of day	Not in a general education school
Students with high-incidence special needs: • Specific learning disabilities • Speech or language impairments • Intellectual disabilities (mild to moderate) • Emotional disturbance				
Students with low-incidence special needs: • Multiple disabilities • Hearing impairments • Orthopedic impairments • Other health impairments • Visual impairments • Autism				

Recent trends: Guiding questions

Indicator	Data
Number of new referrals for special education in the past 3–5 years	
Grade-level differences in achievement of students with special needs on state and local assessments	
Percentage of time students with high-incidence special needs spent in general education classroom for the past 3–5 years	
Percentage of time students with low-incidence special needs spent in general education classroom for the past 3–5 years	

Tool 6.1. Sample snapshot of inclusive education.   *(continued)*

Leadership Strategies for Successful Schoolwide Inclusion: The STAR Approach by Dennis D. Munk & Thomas L. Dempsey
Copyright © 2010 by Paul H. Brookes Publishing Co., Inc. All rights reserved.

Tool 6.1. *(continued)*

Achievement of students with special needs

Measure of achievement	Reading (%)	Math (%)
Meets cutoffs for adequate yearly progress		
Meets benchmarks on local assessments		

Students meeting behavioral expectations

Indicator	Total number for school or district	Number of cases involving students with special needs
Office referrals		
In-school suspension		
Out-of-school suspension		
Placement in alternative or more restrictive placement		

Social participation

Cocurricular participation	Percentage of student body involved	Percentage of students with special needs who are involved
Clubs, organizations, groups, or intramurals for which participation is voluntary		

Leadership Strategies for Successful Schoolwide Inclusion: The STAR Approach by Dennis D. Munk & Thomas L. Dempsey
Copyright © 2010 by Paul H. Brookes Publishing Co., Inc. All rights reserved.

needs on large-scale assessments, the number of office referrals for behavior, and the extent to which students participate in the social life of the school via cocurricular activities. For these outcomes, we recommend looking at the incidence rate for the entire school; for students with special needs, determine whether all students are having the same school experience.

Suggestions for Using Tool 6.1

This tool includes only objective data as a first step so that stakeholders are all starting with a snapshot of placements and common outcomes in their district. Users may wish to take time to expand the scope of their snapshot to include additional outcome data or perception data collected through surveys or program evaluations. Completing a snapshot for your school might be an activity for *Setting the Tone* in the STAR organizer if you are highlighting the importance of inclusive placements and outcomes or *Reflecting on Processes and Outcomes* if you are interested in capturing changes in your school or district.

CREATING A VISION STATEMENT (TOOL 6.2)

Setting the Tone is a logical first step in building or enhancing your inclusive program; creating a vision statement is an ideal activity to be included in your STAR organizer. As discussed in Chapter 2, an important process for developing and approving a vision statement involves staff, students, and parents collaborating to clarify and articulate the underlying beliefs and values that form the foundation for strategic planning and improvement over time. Although there are various formats for writing a vision statement, one of the initial leadership tasks should be the

---

Our school continuously works to engage stakeholders in creating a safe learning environment with high expectations for all students. Our students, staff, and parents continuously work to create a community in which unique individual qualities are valued and recognized as the basis for academic and social success.

Our students
- Value and accept individual differences
- Encourage all classmates to stay socially connected as respected members of our community
- Achieve academic success through responsible learning habits
- Demonstrate creative problem-solving skills

Our staff
- Model inclusive behavior through team planning and problem solving
- Provide opportunities for students to understand how human diversity contributes to creativity and personal accomplishment
- Teach and expect positive social behavior
- Design lessons that consider the learning needs of all students in the classroom
- Continuously monitor student learning and social interaction

Our parents
- Teach inclusive values to their children and encourage them to interact with and accept the differences of others
- Model and reinforce the work habits necessary for academic achievement
- Participate directly in shaping school policies and practices that guide our school environment
- Maintain a close team relationship with teachers and other school staff to support success for their child

---

Tool 6.2. Sample vision statement.

creation of this list of beliefs that will guide subsequent school improvement activities. In reality, school leadership teams are faced with implementing action plans that merge several major initiatives (e.g., curriculum, assessment, positive behavior supports). Identifying inclusive education as a key value ensures that efforts to achieve the highest academic standards will embody the needs of all students, including those with disabilities or other learning differences.

Suggestions for Using Tool 6.2

As part of the self-assessment phase of planning, invite students, staff, and parents to respond to key questions that might lead to developing a clear vision statement with a strong consensus from the community. This might take the form of brief survey questions, input from existing student and parent organizations, and faculty meeting discussions. Allow opportunities for brief, focused discussions on questions, such as the following:

1. What would visitors to our school observe that would indicate that students value and respect individual differences?

2. What would visitors see as evidence that teachers plan instruction to meet the needs of individual students?

3. What comments would we like to hear from parents regarding high achievement results or social belonging for all students, including those with language, learning, or cultural differences?

Include the vision statement on all planning documents and tools so that these values are constantly reflected in action plans over time. Use the vision statement when designing methods to monitor long-term program development. Because key beliefs and values guide initial planning, it makes sense to gather data on whether the action plans are in fact bringing that vision to life for the students in your school. Post the vision statement, along with other key school improvement documents, on the school's web site so that the community can support the values that guide your leadership strategies.

APPLICATIONS OF THE STAR ORGANIZER (TOOLS 6.3–6.5)

In Chapters 1 and 2, we described inclusive education as ever-evolving and best achieved through continuous reflection and improvement. The role of leadership is to guide and support a host of activities that together constitute an inclusive program. Furthermore, leaders must be attuned to research in the four areas of practice captured in STAR and serve as a model for others to focus on these areas. Thus, the strategy can be used for a variety of purposes and by different stakeholders.

The following are three tools for using the STAR organizer, arranged from the simplest form (a blank organizer for leading a meeting or recording decisions made by teams) to a more structured form that can be used to monitor progress on specific activities, to a more comprehensive self-assessment that includes guiding questions. These tools are designed to help focus discussions, clarify priorities, and guide planning.

Blank STAR Organizer (Tool 6.3)

The STAR Organizer is designed to prompt attention to four practice areas critical to inclusive education. The basic organizer can be used to structure discussion at a meeting or as a template for documenting planned activities. The image may be projected or copied as a transparency and filled in during a meeting to save time.

STAR ORGANIZER

AREA OF PRACTICE	SAMPLE LEADERSHIP ACTIVITIES
S *Setting the tone*	
T *Translating research into practice*	
A *Arranging for collaboration*	
R *Reflecting on processes and outcomes*	

Tool 6.3. Blank STAR organizer.

Leadership Strategies for Successful Schoolwide Inclusion: The STAR Approach by Dennis D. Munk & Thomas L. Dempsey
Copyright © 2010 by Paul H. Brookes Publishing Co., Inc. All rights reserved.

STAR Organizer with Leaders and Target Dates (Tool 6.4)

The STAR organizer is intended to use in planning and ongoing monitoring of your inclusive program. Tool 6.4 is a modified organizer that allows assignment of activities to responsible leaders and selection of a target date for completion. Teams may choose to complete the organizer while meeting, with copies for each participant, or project the organizer electronically.

STAR Organizer Self-Assessment Tool (Tool 6.5)

As discussed at various points in the book, the STAR Leadership Strategy was designed for use at different levels of school leadership, and for purposes ranging from strategic planning, to program evaluation, to problem solving. In Chapter 2, we introduced the STAR organizer for identifying leadership activities and guiding questions intended to prompt attention to recommended practices. Here, we provide a tool designed to expedite a self-assessment in each of the four practice areas of STAR, with spaces to record the type of evidence/data used, interpretation of what was found, and what follow-up action is recommended at this time. Our intent was to design a tool that could be used, as is, for formal or informal assessment of your inclusive program, with the expectation that readers may want to individualize their own form to expand writing space or add additional columns (e.g., add columns for target dates and responsible persons). Of course, users might choose to add guiding questions that are more specific to their district or school.

This tool is designed to guide individual leaders or teams through a self-assessment of progress in the four areas of critical practice addressed in the STAR organizer. The tool includes the following components:

1. *Guiding questions:* These questions are designed to focus attention on specific actions and outcomes in each of the practice areas. Guiding questions are appropriate for leadership activities because they direct leaders to focus on specific actions and outcomes while also respecting the fact that schools adopt different structures and strategies for implementing inclusive practices. Each of the four tools includes space for users to construct questions unique to their school or program that will help them understand how well they are meeting goals developed as part of other initiatives (e.g., school improvement plan) but that are related to the quality of their inclusive education program.

2. *Assessment method:* The second column prompts users to record the procedures and evidence they have, or need, to answer the guiding questions. Both formal and informal methods may be used to collect information needed to answer guiding questions. Information that is gathered systematically and from multiple sources is considered most valid and reliable.

3. *Results:* The third column prompts users to record what information they have collected that answers the guiding question. The self-assessment process may reflect positive progress, but may also reveal areas in need of action. Users will have more confidence in their findings if they follow a systematic and thorough procedure for collecting information.

4. *Recommended actions:* The last column involves actually completing the STAR organizer by constructing activities for each of the four practice areas. Having completed the four tools, users may observe common themes across areas that can be addressed in one activity.

STAR ORGANIZER

AREA OF PRACTICE	SAMPLE LEADERSHIP ACTIVITIES	RESPONSIBLE LEADER	TARGET DATE
S *Setting the tone*			
T *Translating research into practice*			
A *Arranging for collaboration*			
R *Reflecting on processes and outcomes*			

Tool 6.4. The STAR organizer with leaders and target dates.

Leadership Strategies for Successful Schoolwide Inclusion: The STAR Approach by Dennis D. Munk & Thomas L. Dempsey
Copyright © 2010 by Paul H. Brookes Publishing Co., Inc. All rights reserved.

SETTING THE TONE

Guiding questions	How did we assess?	What did we find out?	What actions are recommended?
How does our school vision acknowledge a commitment to inclusiveness and to the success of all learners?			
How well is our mission and vision understood by the entire school community?			
How do members of the school community demonstrate equality and respect in the way they talk to and about learners with diverse abilities and needs?			
How do school personnel demonstrate their shared responsibility for the success of all learners?			
How and when does the decision-making process for the school take into account the impact for learners with diverse needs?			
How do we ensure that students with diverse needs feel they are valued as members of the school community?			
Your questions:			

Tool 6.5. The STAR organizer self-assessment tool. *(continued)*

Leadership Strategies for Successful Schoolwide Inclusion: The STAR Approach by Dennis D. Munk & Thomas L. Dempsey
Copyright © 2010 by Paul H. Brookes Publishing Co., Inc. All rights reserved.

Tool 6.5. *(continued)*

TRANSLATING RESEARCH INTO PRACTICE

Guiding questions	How did we assess?	What did we find out?	What actions are recommended?
How do we use data to determine which of our current practices are successful and should be used more consistently across inclusive classrooms?			
How do we learn about new practices that could be helpful in our school?			
How do we learn what types of professional development the educational teams need?			
How do we support teams in implementing a new practice?			
How do we ensure that new practices found to be effective are shared with the entire school and sustained over time?			
Your questions:			

Leadership Strategies for Successful Schoolwide Inclusion: The STAR Approach by Dennis D. Munk & Thomas L. Dempsey
Copyright © 2010 by Paul H. Brookes Publishing Co., Inc. All rights reserved.

ARRANGING FOR COLLABORATION

Guiding questions	How did we assess?	What did we find out?	What actions are recommended?
How important do staff members perceive collaboration to be at our school?			
How do we take full advantage of the expertise of the teachers and specialists?			
What opportunities exist for team members to collaborate about how to instruct and support learners with special needs?			
When do the general and special educators plan together for instruction in an inclusive classroom?			
When do general and special education teachers coteach in a general education classroom?			
How does our school engage parents as partners in maintaining an inclusive delivery model?			
Your questions:			

(continued)

Leadership Strategies for Successful Schoolwide Inclusion: The STAR Approach by Dennis D. Munk & Thomas L. Dempsey
Copyright © 2010 by Paul H. Brookes Publishing Co., Inc. All rights reserved.

Tool 6.5. *(continued)*

REFLECTING ON PROCESSES AND OUTCOMES

Guiding questions	How did we assess?	What did we find out?	What actions are recommended?
How do teams determine whether all learners are making progress in an inclusive classroom?			
How do teams adjust when learners are not making progress? What types of data do we use to ensure we are providing maximum access and maximum participation?			
How and when do we solicit input from students and parents about the quality of our program?			
How and when do we evaluate our program for presence of recommended practices?			
How would we know if a learner was not experiencing academic or social success in our school?			
Your questions:			

Leadership Strategies for Successful Schoolwide Inclusion: The STAR Approach by Dennis D. Munk & Thomas L. Dempsey
Copyright © 2010 by Paul H. Brookes Publishing Co., Inc. All rights reserved.

Recommendations from the four tools may be prioritized for short-term and longer term action. Each column of guiding questions includes space for users to add questions relevant to their own school.

SAMPLE PROFESSIONAL DEVELOPMENT SURVEY (TOOL 6.6)

Professional development is key to implementing any new program or practice, and it should be considered vital to effective inclusive education and a leadership activity for your STAR organizer. In the STAR Leadership Strategy, the role of professional development is most obvious in the practice area of *Translating Research into Practice*. In Chapter 2, we discussed research-based strategies for designing, implementing, and evaluating professional development activities, beginning with involving educational teams in decisions regarding topics and the format in which expertise will be shared. As discussed in Chapter 2, teachers are more likely to adopt new practices if they perceive that these changes will help them be more successful with challenging students.

Surveying staff about what knowledge and skills they would like to learn more about through professional development is one way of revealing their questions and concerns. A complementary approach to prioritizing development needs is to assess the extent to which staff embrace, understand, and implement the basic elements of your school vision. Professional development may be needed to ensure that all staff understand the importance of core beliefs, such as an assumption that all students can learn, and the responsibility for all learners is shared by the entire school. Tool 6.6 includes items intended to assess underlying beliefs, as well as solicit priorities for development on specific topics or practices. Survey questions are relatively easy to design and provide easy-to-gather data on the perceptions of staff, parents, or students. The substance and format of the survey can be altered to fit the needs of your particular school as one of the ongoing tasks carried out by the leadership team or professional development committee. Participants are asked to indicate their professional role so that results for each role can be disaggregated later. This section might also be arranged to identify respondents in other categories (e.g., grade level, department, team) according to the parameters selected for analysis. The sample we have included is designed to assess beliefs and current practice on a number of issues related to inclusive practice. Examples of multiple choice and open-ended questions are included as well. We recommend the use of an online protocol for administering surveys (e.g., http://www.surveymonkey.com) for both expedience and efficiency in summarizing the results.

Suggestions for Using Tool 6.6

Before finalizing a written action plan, the school leadership team may wish to identify those action steps that can be monitored by periodic collection of survey data. If possible, combine items from across action strategies into one survey to be administered at predetermined times. Typically, survey data is collected at the beginning and end of each school year—or at a minimum, once annually.

If it is important to compare responses from different groups within the staff or school community, be sure to design the survey so that you can analyze results easily by the respondent groups you wish to compare.

Share the results in a timely manner. Survey results often lead people to engage in dialogue that contributes positively to problem solving and the development of new ideas for improvement.

School: _____   Date: _____

Please check the one that best describes your role:

__ General classroom teacher   __ Special education teacher   __ Related services staff
__ Administrator/supervisor   __ Bilingual/ESL teacher   __ Guidance counselor
__ Academic/behavior coach   __ Parent   __ Other (specify) _____

Directions: Your responses to the following items are important in shaping the professional development priorities in our school for the coming year. Please respond to each item.	Strongly disagree	Disagree	Agree	Strongly agree	No opinion
1. All students can meet standards in the general education curriculum if they receive high-quality instruction.					
Reflects my belief					
Reflects current practice in our school					
2. Teachers should be responsible for differentiating instruction within courses to meet the diverse needs of our student body.					
Reflects my belief					
Reflects current practice in our school					
3. Students with mild to moderate disabilities (e.g., learning disabilities) should be taught as much as possible in the general education classroom with the needed supports and accommodations.					
Reflects my belief					
Reflects current practice in our school					
4. Students with more severe disabilities (e.g., intellectual disabilities) should be taught as much as possible in the general education classroom with the needed supports and accommodations.					
Reflects my belief					
Reflects current practice in our school					
5. Teachers should alter classroom instruction if assessment data indicate that a significant number of students are performing poorly.					
Reflects my belief					
Reflects current practice in our school					

Tool 6.6. Sample professional development survey.

Leadership Strategies for Successful Schoolwide Inclusion: The STAR Approach by Dennis D. Munk & Thomas L. Dempsey
Copyright © 2010 by Paul H. Brookes Publishing Co., Inc. All rights reserved.

	Strongly disagree	Disagree	Agree	Strongly agree	No opinion
6. Parents should actively participate in the design of our school's special education service delivery model.					
Reflects my belief					
Reflects current practice in our school					
7. Teachers should be provided with training on specialized adaptations that enhance success in the general education setting for students with disabilities.					
Reflects my belief					
Reflects current practice in our school					
8. The practice of using zeroes (on a 100-point scale) for missing work is a fair method for teachers to use in assigning student grades.					
Reflects my belief					
Reflects current practice in our school					

9. Please select the top three priorities you believe are needed to maximize school improvement.

Check 3 priorities below

Tier 1 strategies for differentiating instruction	
Evidence-based supplemental/intensive reading interventions	
Evidence-based supplemental/intensive math interventions	
Schoolwide behavior systems	
Classroom adaptations for learners with special needs	
Other (please specify)	

10. What is the most important professional development need in your school for the next 2 years?

Leadership Strategies for Successful Schoolwide Inclusion: The STAR Approach by Dennis D. Munk & Thomas L. Dempsey
Copyright © 2010 by Paul H. Brookes Publishing Co., Inc. All rights reserved.

Use the results and subsequent dialogue to revise your action plan when changes are needed. As systemic changes occur (whether positive or negative), so do the perceptions of key stakeholders in the school. This is vital information for successful planning by the school leadership team.

PARENT SURVEY DESCRIPTION (TOOL 6.7)

The importance of involving parents in decision making regarding inclusion was discussed in Chapter 3, in which strategies for maximizing involvement and satisfaction were provided. Parents of children with IEPs should be considered part of the team who are capable of providing helpful feedback on your overall program and their child's IEP process. Soliciting parent feedback on a routine basis allows you to react quickly to concerns. It can prevent the building of concerns to a point where anger and frustration interfere with your ability to engage in problem solving. Surveying parent satisfaction is a recommended activity for your STAR organizer.

Parent input is critical for monitoring the quality of services, as well as the extent to which students and parents feel included as members of the school community and as partners in designing an individualized education plan. In addition, inviting parents to complete a survey once or twice annually provides a basis for ongoing dialogue through advisory groups, PTA/PTO groups, or parent support networks. The underlying principle is that continuous improvement is the goal and parents are valued as partners in that effort. The sample parent survey in Tool 6.7 is one example of a format that uses a rating scale in combination with at least one open-ended question to assess parents' perception on the quality of services, inclusive practice, and parent partnership. Categories and specific survey items can be modified to capture the critical perceptions of parents on key issues that have been identified by the leadership team.

Suggestions for Using Tool 6.7

Before designing a survey to be distributed to parents, determine the key factors that are critical to monitor over time. The sample survey is organized around three factors (quality, inclusiveness, and parent partnership) that the leadership team has determined are important building blocks for the special education service delivery model. Review existing formal or informal data, and encourage the team to identify the specific survey items based on the needs of your school.

Design your survey to balance simplicity and specificity. More specific, nonambiguous questions are more likely to yield useful perception data. Also be aware of "hot button" issues in the school community. Be clear that you are seeking honest input on policy or practice, but take care to avoid setting up questions that lead respondents to offer personal criticism of staff or administrators.

Consider a survey that samples opinions from parents, students, and staff on beliefs or best practice that correlate with high-quality inclusive education. This could afford school leaders with a program-monitoring tool that could cross-tabulate data from all three groups at specified intervals over time.

IEP MEETING FEEDBACK (TOOL 6.8)

In Chapter 4, we discussed strategies for enhancing the IEP process, including maximizing general educator participation, maximizing student participation, and clarifying how sup-

School: _____ Date: _____	Strongly disagree	Disagree	Agree	Strongly agree	No opinion
Directions: Your responses to the following items will provide us with valuable input on how our school can improve special education service delivery. Please answer each item.					
Quality of services					
1. My child is making acceptable academic progress.					
2. The classroom teacher understands the needs of my child.					
3. My child's critical educational needs are listed in the IEP.					
4. My child receives the supports/services listed in the IEP.					
5. My child's progress on IEP goals is communicated clearly and regularly.					
Inclusive practice					
6. Students with special needs should be taught primarily in the general education classroom.					
7. My child receives the supports needed to be successful in the general education classroom.					
8. My child is taught the same curriculum as other students.					
9. General and special educators work together to ensure that my child's IEP is being implemented.					
10. My child feels that he/she is a valued member of the classroom and school community.					
Parent partnership					
11. Concerns I have about my child's IEP are resolved effectively.					
12. Necessary information about my child's needs in school is communicated to me in a timely way.					
13. I am considered an equal partner with teachers and other professionals in planning my child's educational program.					
14. I have been asked my opinion about how well special education services are meeting my child's needs.					
15. School staff try to ensure that I fully understand the procedural safeguards (parent rights).					

Other suggestions/comments:

Tool 6.7. Sample parent survey for parents of students with individualized education programs (IEPs).

Leadership Strategies for Successful Schoolwide Inclusion: The STAR Approach by Dennis D. Munk & Thomas L. Dempsey
Copyright © 2010 by Paul H. Brookes Publishing Co., Inc. All rights reserved.

Your title:				
Name: (optional)	Month:	School:		Grade:

Please take a few moments to reflect on today's IEP meeting. We strongly believe that an efficient meeting process leads to effective teams and better results for students.

	Yes	No
1. This meeting covered the topics I wanted to discuss.		
2. IEP issues were resolved to my satisfaction.		
3. The process was efficient and time was used well.		
4. The IEP team valued my input.		
5. The level of involvement for my child/student was appropriate.		
6. We discussed how to maximize my child's/student's participation in general education.		

Additional comments or suggestions:

Tool 6.8. Sample individualized education program (IEP) meeting feedback form.

Leadership Strategies for Successful Schoolwide Inclusion: The STAR Approach by Dennis D. Munk & Thomas L. Dempsey
Copyright © 2010 by Paul H. Brookes Publishing Co., Inc. All rights reserved.

ports can best be used to support achievement in the general curriculum. The IEP meeting represents the culmination of those efforts. The way in which the meeting is conducted can validate or undermine hard work preparing for the meeting. In Chapter 3, we discussed the importance of involving parents in your inclusive program. For those parents who have children with IEPs, that involvement should include the IEP process and culminating meeting. Thus, evaluating the quality of your meetings is an ideal activity for you to include in your STAR organizer.

When professionals and parents behave inclusively, their students are more likely to do so. In the eyes of many parents and school staff, how an IEP meeting is conducted is critically important to the development of a strong educational plan that is most likely to have a positive outcome for the individual student involved. Meetings that are well planned and well facilitated are more likely to build the team collaboration necessary to establish trust and sustain high-quality inclusive education. Tool 6.8 provides a method for frequent monitoring of the extent to which participants perceive that the IEP process models inclusive practice; it is effective and efficient for making sound educational decisions. As outlined in Chapter 4, many IEP teams find that best practice often means going beyond procedural requirements in order to address the intangibles of human interaction—a necessary skill set for effective teams. Although disagreements are inevitable in some cases, there is a greater likelihood that conflicts will be resolved when participants feel their knowledge and expertise are respected during the meeting process. This monitoring tool is designed for brief, frequent collection of qualitative data on the IEP meeting process. It should be tailored to contain the specific variables most pertinent to the needs of each school or district.

Suggestions for Using Tool 6.8

Customize the content to target specific stakeholders (e.g., parents) or provide all team members with the opportunity to complete the form. Of course, more stakeholders will require more time for data management.

Make the survey fit the needs of your school or team. If, for example, you have reason to believe that parents feel their opinions are not always valued, that could be a specific variable to include in the assessment tool.

The survey can be completed on paper, sent and returned as an e-mail attachment, or posted online at the end of each semester using your district web site or a survey web site (e.g., http://www.surveymonkey.com).

You can also alter the survey to use a rating scale rather than *yes* or *no* responses. Responses can be disaggregated by title, school, grade level or individual issue. This may be most easily accomplished through online data collection two or three times per school year so that responses are automatically calculated using predetermined parameters.

After data have been collected and summarized, include this information in leadership team meetings for continuous monitoring of your school's long-term plan. If warranted, use this data set to develop action steps for the IEP process, and continue to monitor progress on these specific issues during the coming school year.

SAMPLE PROGRAM MONITORING (TOOL 6.9)

Reflecting on Processes and Outcomes can include both informal and formal program evaluation. In Chapter 2, we provide two examples of published instruments for evaluating an inclusive education program. In this chapter, we provide a tool for self-assessing your program using

School:			Date:		
Program component	Evaluation question	Data source	**Rating**	Next steps
			1 = Not started 2 = Progressing 3 = Implemented	

Tool 6.9. Sample program monitoring tool.

Leadership Strategies for Successful Schoolwide Inclusion: The STAR Approach by Dennis D. Munk & Thomas L. Dempsey
Copyright © 2010 by Paul H. Brookes Publishing Co., Inc. All rights reserved.

the guiding questions for STAR (Tool 6.5). Tool 6.9 is a more generic tool for program evaluation that can be individualized to fit your unique needs. The importance of ongoing reflection and evaluation is discussed in numerous places in this book, and it is more likely to occur with a tool that is easy to implement.

For school leaders to successfully implement action plans, they will need a method for monitoring the extent to which plans are being carried out as designed and whether or not the intended objectives have been met. In short, they must continuously reflect on outcomes. Too often, good ideas fail—not because they were ill conceived, but because of poor implementation or lack of needed adjustments throughout the school year. Tool 6.9 can be adapted for the specific needs of your school as you engage teams to gather and share ongoing data to determine if change efforts are on track. For each program component or action strategy, specific monitoring questions and data sources should be formulated during the initial development of the action plan so that the outcomes for each strategy can be assessed at predetermined intervals. One or more data sources are listed for each strategy, along with team ratings and next steps to be taken. It is critical that ratings and next steps are recorded only by consensus of the leadership team during a meeting in which data are discussed and analyzed.

Suggestions for Using Tool 6.9

When the leadership team develops a written long-term plan, that plan should specify data that will be collected to assess the implementation level and effectiveness of action steps. These data are then summarized in Tool 6.9 at specified intervals. Gather and summarize baseline data using this tool at the inception of the school improvement or action plan. Follow up at the end of the semester or school year to assess progress for each program component.

Leadership teams should complete the ratings and determine next steps as part of the team meeting process. This should be done electronically for easy completion and distribution. Specific data collection and summarizing could be assigned to individual team members to maximize efficiency.

Share this completed tool in a timely way with staff, parents, and (when appropriate) students. Use the results as a springboard for celebration and problem solving during grade-level, department, or faculty meetings. Adapt the format to meet the needs of your team or school. The main purpose is to gather ongoing data on predetermined outcomes so that adjustments can be made when needed.

Index

Information in boxes, figures, and tables is indicated by *b, f,* and *t,* respectively.

Academic choice, 84*b*
Academic support, 84*b*
Access
  conditions of, 81*t*
  definition of, 80
  elements of, 81*t*
  maximization of, 82, 87*f*
Access to general curriculum, 79–86
Accommodations
  balancing of, 68–69, 71*f*
  examples of, 70*t*
  grading and, 70*t*
  purpose of, 70*t*
  STAR organizer for, 71*f*
Achievement, leadership and, 38
Action, multiple means of, 88*t*
Activities
  for balancing accommodations and modifications, 71*f*
  for collaboration, 17*f*
  for maximizing general educator participation in IEP, 62*f*
  for monitoring progress in general education curriculum, 69*f*
  for reflection, 17*f*
  for tone setting, 16*f*
  for translating research into practice, 16*f*
Administrator roles, 40–44
Alternative teaching, 22
Areas of practice, 1–2
Assumptions, critical, 2
Authentic assessments, 67

Borrowed time, 25*t*
Brown v. Board of Education, 7

Case study, in STAR leadership, 32–35
Center for Applied Special Technology, 88
Choice, academic, 84*b*
ChoiceMaker Self-Determination Curriculum, 72
Collaboration
  access and, 87*f*
  arrangements for, 22
  community, 50*t*
  individualized education program (IEP) and, 62*f,* 66*f*
  peer supports and, 47*f*

  in STAR leadership strategy, 15, 17*f,* 20–23, 23*t,* 31*f*
  strategies for, 24*t*
  time for, 25*t*
  universal design for learning and, 91*f*
Commitment, implementation and, 2
Common time, 25*t*
Communication with parents, 50*t*
Community, sense of, 84*b*
Community collaboration, 50*t*
Component rating scale, 28*t*–29*t,* 30–31
Conditions of access, 81*t*
Conflict, individualized education program (IEP) facilitation and, 74
Context, 3–9
Coplanning, 23*t,* 24*t*
Coteaching, 22
Culture, collaborative, 20–21, 24*t*
Curriculum, definition of, 80

Decision making
  in individualized education program (IEP), 85*f*
  with parents, 50*t*
Design for learning, universal, 86–90, 88*t,* 91*f*
Diagnostic instruction, 93*t*
Digital text, 88

Education for All Handicapped Children Act of 1975, 1, 7
Educational teams, definition of, 3
Encouragement, 84*b*
Engagement
  access and, 81*t*
  multiple means of, 88*t*
Environment, least restrictive, 4–5
Evidence-based practices, 19
Exposure, access and, 81*t*
Expression, multiple means of, 88*t*

Failing grades, 86
Fairness, 18
Forms, individualized education program (IEP), 67
Found time, 25*t*
Freed-up time, 25*t*
Friendship, peer, 44–47

General curriculum, definition of, 80
General education
    definition of, 3
    maximizing access to, 79–86
    participation in individualized education program
        (IEP), 60–61, 60b
    time spent in, 4t, 5t
Good High Schools project, 82, 84b
Grading, 85–86

Historical context, 6–9
Historical research, 10t
Home learning, 50t

IDEA, see Individuals with Disabilities Education
        Improvement Act of 2004
IEP, see Individualized education program
Implementation, commitment and, 2
Inclusion
    components rating scale, 28t–29t, 30–31
    context for, 3–9
    definition of, 1, 3
    goals for, 82
    in Individuals with Disabilities Education
        Improvement Act (IDEA) of 2004, 5–6, 6t
    in No Child Left Behind Act (NCLB) of 2001,
        5–6, 6t
    perspective on, 2–3
    physical, 4
    snapshot of, 101–104
Individualized education program (IEP)
    access in, 80
    aligning with general curriculum, 61–67, 66f
    balancing of accommodations and modifications,
        68–69, 70t
    collaboration and, 62f, 66f
    decision making process for, 85f
    facilitation, 74
    forms, 67
    general educator participation in, 60–61, 60b
    goals in, 65–66
    guidelines, 59–61
    in Individuals with Disabilities Education
        Improvement Act (IDEA) of 2004, 57, 59–61
    lack of research on, 57
    meeting feedback tool, 116–119
    parent experiences with, 58
    progress monitoring, 67
    reflection and, 62f, 66f
    research on, 59
    self-directed, 71–73, 73f
    standards-based, 63, 63f, 64f, 65–66, 65t
    student experiences with, 58
    student involvement with, 70–74
    teacher experiences with, 58
    teams, definition of, 3
    tone setting and, 62f, 66f
    universal design for learning and, 90
Individuals with Disabilities Education Improvement
        Act (IDEA) of 2004

    access in, 79–80
    individualized education program (IEP) in, 57, 59–61
    inclusion in, 5–6, 6t
    least restrictive environment in, 4–5
    No Child Left Behind Act (NCLB) of 2001 vs, 6t
Institute of Education Sciences, 20b
Intervention, response to, 90–94
Iowa Test of Basic Skills, 9

Leadership, 9–10
    achievement and, 38
    collaboration and, 21, 23
    elements of, 10–11
    principal, 37–40, 39t
    responsive, 84b
    see also STAR leadership strategy access and, 80–81
Leadership strategy, 1–2
Learning Disabilities Research & Practice, 84b
Learning standards, 63, 63f
Least restrictive environment, 4–5
Low grades, 86

Maximization of access, 82
Modifications
    balancing of, 68–69, 71f
    examples of, 70t
    grading and, 70t
    purpose of, 70t
    STAR organizer for, 71f
Monitoring progress, 67–68
Monitoring protocol, 42

National Center for Education Research, 19
National Instructional Materials Accessibility Stan-
        dard, 88
NCLB, see No Child Left Behind Act of 2001
New time, 25t
No Child Left Behind (NCLB) Act of 2001, 2
    evidence-based practices and, 19
    general curriculum access in, 80
    Individuals with Disabilities Education
        Improvement Act (IDEA) of 2004 vs, 6t
    inclusion in, 5–6, 6t
    parent involvement and, 48

Oberti v. Board of Education of the Borough of Clementon
        School District, 4–5
Office of Special Education Programs, 88
Outcomes, reflecting on, 23–31

Parallel teaching, 22
Parenting, 50t
Parents
    communication, 50t
    experiences with individualized education
        programs (IEPs), 58
    involvement, 48–51, 50t

questions, 49
    survey, 116
    in vision statement, 104
    volunteers, 50*t*
Participation, 84*b*
Peer Buddy programs, 46*f*
Peer friendship, 44–47
Perspective, on inclusive education, 2–3
Physical inclusion, 4
Planning time, 25*t*
PQMT, *see* Program Quality Measurement Tool
Practice(s)
    areas of, 1–2
    classwide, 2–3
    schoolwide, 2
    in STAR leadership strategy, 15
Principal leadership, 37–40, 39*t*
Processes, reflecting on, 23–31
Professional development needs survey, 113–116
Program monitoring tool, 119–121
Program Quality Measurement Tool (PQMT), 25, 26*t*–27*t*
Progress, access and, 81*t*
Progress monitoring, 67–68
Purchased time, 25*t*

Questions
    for administrators, 41, 42, 43, 44
    in collaboration, 31*f*
    for general educators with an included learner, 61*b*
    of parents, 49
    in reflection, 24, 31*f*
    in research translation, 30*f*
    in standards-based individualized education
        program (IEP) development, 64*f*
    in tone setting, 30*f*

Reflection
    access and, 87*f*
    individualized education program (IEP) and, 62*f*, 66*f*
    parent involvement and, 52*f*
    peer supports and, 47*f*
    questions in, 24
    in STAR leadership strategy, 15, 17*f*, 23–31, 31*f*
    strategies for, 26*t*
    time for, 25*t*
    universal design for learning and, 91*f*
Regular Education Initiative, 7
Released time, 25*t*
Representation, multiple means of, 88*t*
Rescheduled time, 25*t*
Research, 8–9, 10*t*
    access and, 87*f*
    on individualized education programs (IEPs), 59
    on individualized education program (IEPs), lack
        of, 57
    peer supports and, 47*f*
    skepticism on, 21*t*
    in STAR leadership strategy, 15, 16*f*, 18–20, 30*f*

    translation of, 21*t*
    universal design for learning and, 91*f*
Response to intervention (RTI), 90–94
Responsive leadership, 84*b*
Retention, 40
Roles, administrator, 40–44
RTI, *see* Response to intervention

*Sacramento City Unified School District Board of Educa-
    tion v. Rachel H.,* 5
Screening, universal, 93*t*
Segregation, 7–8
Self-assessment tool, 107–113
Self-directed individualized education program (IEP),
    71–73, 73*f*
Skepticism, on research, 21*t*
SMARTER planning process, 82, 83*f*
Snapshot of inclusion, 101–104
Special needs learners, definition of, 3
Specialized instruction, 93*t*
Standards-based grading, 86
Standards-based individualized education program
    (IEP), 64*f*
Standards-based reform, 63
STAR leadership strategy
    case study in, 32–35
    collaboration in, 15, 17*f*, 20–23, 23*t*, 31*f*
    implementation of, 31–32
    practices of, 15
    for principal leadership, 45*f*
    reflection in, 15, 17*f*, 23–31, 31*f*
    research in, 15, 16*f*, 18–20, 21*t*, 30*f*
    tone in, 15, 16–18, 16*f*, 18*t*, 30*f*
STAR organizer
    for aligning individualized education program
        (IEP) with general curriculum, 66*t*
    applications of, 105–113
    blank, 105–106, 108
    for implementing response to intervention (RTI),
        97*t*
    for implementing universal design for learning, 91*t*
    with leaders and target dates, 107
    for maximizing access to general education
        curriculum, 87*t*
    for maximizing general educator participation in
        IEP process, 62*t*
    for maximizing parent involvement, 52*t*
    for maximizing peer supports, 47*t*
    for maximizing student involvement in the IEP
        process, 72*t*
    for monitoring progress in general education
        curriculum, 69*t*
    self-assessment tool, 107–113
    for strategically balancing accommodations and
        modifications, 71*t*
Station teaching, 22
Student involvement with individualized education
    program (IEP), 70–74, 73*f*
Student-Led IEPs: A Guide for Student Involvement
    (McGahee, Mason, Wallace, & Jones), 73
Supplemental instruction, 93*t*

Support
   academic, 84b
   peer, 44–47
Supporting roles, 43–44
Supporting strategies, 7t
Survey
   parent, 116
   professional development needs, 113–116

Teacher retention, 40
Teacher turnover, 40
Team teaching, 22
Terminology, 3
Text, digital, 88
Three-tiered system, 92f, 93t, 95f
Tiered time, 25t
Time, strategies for expansion of, 25t
Tone
   access and, 87f
   individualized education program (IEP) and, 62f, 66f
   parent involvement and, 52f
   peer supports and, 47f
   questions for, 30f
   in STAR leadership strategy, 15, 16–18, 16f, 18t, 30f
   strategies for setting, 18t
   universal design for learning and, 91f

Tools
   individualized education program (IEP) meeting feedback, 116–119
   parent survey, 116
   professional development needs survey, 113–116
   program monitoring, 119–121
   self-assessment, 107–113
   snapshot of inclusion, 101–104
   STAR organizer applications, 105–113
   vision statement, 104–105
Translation, of research, 15, 16f, 21t
Turnover, 40

UDL, see Universal design for learning
Undermining strategies, 7t
Universal design for learning, 86–90, 88t, 91f
Universal screening, 93t

Values, critical, 2
Vision statement tool, 104–105
Visioning, 16
Volunteering, 50t

Walking the talk, 40–41
What Works Clearinghouse, 19, 20b